Skinny Bits

Wisdom for a Flourishing Image Business

By

Lynne Marks, AICI, CIM

Illustrated by Kat Martin

Contribution by Jill Bremer

"Skinny Bits: Wisdom for a Flourishing Image Business," by Lynne Henderson Marks, AICI, CIM. ISBN 1-58939-873-4.

Published in the United States of America.

FOREWORD

SKINNY BITS: Wisdom for a Flourishing Image Business.

This book is for consultants or aspiring consultants who want to take their image consulting business to the next level. From my nearly 20 years' experience, I know that successful image consultants are passionate about people, beauty and human beings. They are committed that people grow, flourish and express themselves, from the inside and the outside.

"Human beings are actually created for the transcendent, for the sublime, for the beautiful, for the truthful, and you don't teach people those things. It comes with the package of being human and all of us are given the task of trying to make this world a little more hospitable to these beautiful things- to love, to compassion, to caring, to sharing, just to being human."

Desmond Tutu

I am convinced that what makes a happy life is to contribute to others in some way. In this book I hope you will find at least one "Skinny Bit": A thin morsel of wisdom that you can use for yourself or take away and use, to make a difference in the life of someone. Go fourth and flourish!

Lynne Marks, AICI, CIM
2006

DEDICATION

I would like to dedicate this book to my parents. My wonderful mother taught me the beauty of color, style and fabric and how to make my own clothes when I was eight years old. My Dad made me into an image consultant when I was ten. I was about to go out with my parents when he took one look at my outfit. "I'm not going out with that kid looking like that." he said. And with that, I had to go back into the house and change, knowing that the way I looked must be a very important thing!

ACKNOWLEDGMENTS

I have learned that it takes a village to write a book! I would like to acknowledge all the people who have contributed to this book, whether they know it or not.

First I would like to thank my editor, Iris Gathing, a certified image consultant and graduate of London Image Institute's Executive Course. Her undying patience, technical insights and attention to detail have been inspiring. She literally changed my definition of "grueling" to fun and ease!

Kat Martin the wonderful artist was able to capture the essence of my thoughts and writing in her loving cartoons. They illustrate so brilliantly the *humanity* of the entrepreneurial venture and the despair and exhilaration we all experience on any given day of our lives.

Tracy Keever designed a dramatic cover that caused my whole concept of short, easy to read lite-bites to jump to life. Skinny Bits is a term I invented more than 20 years ago from a fashion design concept, to illustrate how garments need to frame, show or attach themselves to a thin part of the body, thus allowing the proportions of the body to be enhanced.

I would also like to thank Jill Bremer, an AICI colleague for contributing her time, wisdom and energy to writing a chapter of this book. Her experience on book publishing was invaluable and insightful and her chapter is full of relevant, useful information.

Lastly I would like to thank my graduates, my partners over the years, my family and my friends who all contributed their own words of wisdom and didn't even know I was listening! Well I was, and they are all in this book.

CONTENTS

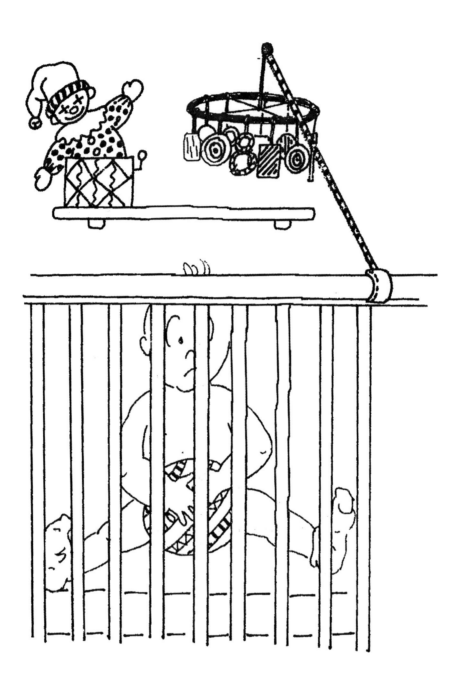

Chapter 1

WHAT IS IMAGE? A NEW VIEW

Imagine yourself as a new born infant in your crib looking out at a hazy world where interesting things are dangled in front of you. You are bundled up all soft and warm, held and touched by people with a familiar smell who are spooning good tasting stuff into your mouth from time to time. Long before you can speak, everything about the world around you, from objects and your physical environment to your fingers and toes, delivers a rich canvas of information. You stick the rattle in your mouth to find out more about it. You stare at something unblinking for many minutes at a time. Without words, the exploration is detailed, fascinating, and intense. What's more, these objects become constant in your world, so you learn to rely on them and everything else you can see, touch, taste, hear and smell. One tiny impression at a time, your *real*

world takes shape and you get pretty upset when things change or disappear.

In the physical world of objects, consider yourself also as a moving object that is to be clothed, fed, and protected. This physical world also includes our *physical infrastructure*, which is everything we can see that either is draped on us or grows out of us. It all becomes the most fundamental, real, persuasive and trustworthy form of communication that exists to human beings. It is transparent, often unnoticed, yet it has shaped our lives from birth, and is critical not only to the way we perceive our world, but also to the way others perceive us. It stays largely in the background and forms the stage and set of our lives, quietly shaping what we call our self-image, or how we define, recognize, and project ourselves, one tiny piece at a time. Millions of messages are created from these perceptions, filed away in memory, and collectively become "the past." It becomes a foundation for the language we use to describe each other.

WHAT EXACTLY IS THE FIRST IMPRESSION?

Fast forward to adulthood and think about what happens when we look at someone for the first time. Realize that by now, we have mastered an automatic mechanism that occurs the moment we see another person. In a flash we constantly perceive, judge, assess, compare, and evaluate each other and ourselves. By nature, we do not approach any meeting with a clean slate.

> *Once distinguished as a communication tool, this non-verbal yet all- powerful language is one we can utilize as image consultants, to bring about lasting changes for our clients.*

And what of the role of language?

In addition to the vast store of nonverbal information, we now have available the verbal communication which adds in a whole new layer of its own! In similar fashion, the verbal language has also been stored away. It now serves to enhance the nonverbal with labels, meanings, and interpretations. Having laid down memories about our own image from a very early age, we now have additional information to help retain and enhance the nonverbal memories. Our nonverbal pictures are interpreted to form a background and experience literally loaded with associations, good, bad, and ugly.

So again, what exactly are we looking for? Similar to any other member of the animal kingdom, we are scanning for threat: to see if you are friend or foe. We make decisions about each other based on what we see. The minute our eyes alight on someone for the very first time, we decide very quickly, what they *are like.* We relate back to that powerful, meaningful world of objects which we have now interpreted! We use it as a short cut to understand people and the world around us. Not a word is spoken, but the picture has been formed, and with it comes all the associations. We have literally created a "radio personality" in our heads that talks to us incessantly about everything we see and hear.

Knowing this, it is not surprising that we put so much credence in the first impression. We are now on the firing line and the brain has work to do! Quick as a wink, we evaluate the nonverbal picture. Our judgments actually stop short the exploration of the nonverbal objects we are about to meet. "Hello" we say, ("I know exactly who you are," we think.) We say, "It's nice to meet you for the very first time!"

Back to Basics

Let's examine briefly how the mind works. Think of the brain as a vast storage device that retains trillions of patterns of data stored by bundles of nerve cells. This information, largely unconscious, always available, and able to be accessed at a moment's notice, provides valuable information to our survival. Interestingly, new research in neuroscience from Dr. Michael I. Posner, an emeritus professor of neuroscience at the University of Oregon and expert on attention, (and others experts), has demonstrated in studies that information from our world is coded and stored by our brain in various ways. For example, raw sensory data from our

senses, touch, taste, sight, sound, and smell employ dedicated neurons to carry patterns of information or *perception memory patterns* to the primary sensory regions of the brain. From there they are carried to higher brain regions where interpretation occurs.

Similarly anything we say, decide or do in any particular situation is also coded in patterns known as *action memory patterns*. This bottom to top flow is known as "feed forward." The neurons are able to make associations with each other top to bottom, bottom to top and side to side. They can be activated instantly at the touch of a switch.

Naturally, one would absolutely expect the brain to be busy taking in and coding all the information that bombards the eyes on a daily basis, but there is another, even more active process at work. Posner found that *top to bottom processing is even busier*. Astoundingly there are 10 times as many nerve fibers interpreting the information in the brain and carrying it back to the conscious mind as thoughts, and then to the eyes as images. Apparently, what we end up seeing is not the same as the actual world, but instead, our perception of the world.

It appears that the final interpretation given back to us is very different from the initial object that is actually seen by the retina. As the brain feeds it back through what we commonly call "filters," the primary object is actually now loaded with interpretations from our experiences and memory patterns, coded in the brain, and pulled down from their shelf with the express function to override any semblance of reality! Posner calls it "top-down processing" which is a mechanism at work at all times for the purpose of prediction and survival of the species. Why would we need that function? Simply put, if we are given information in advance of danger, such as other situations or people who have threatened us before, we can *predict* threat and are in a much better position to take action and protect ourselves. That also goes for anyone we meet. "Top-down processes override sensory, or bottom-up information," says Dr. Stephen M. Kosslyn, a neuroscientist from Harvard. "People think that sights,

sounds, and touch from the outside world constitute reality. But the brain constructs what it perceives, based on past experience." *New York Times: "This is Your Brain under Hypnosis" by Sandra Blakeslee. November 22, 2005*

Once it perceives threat or danger, the part of the brain that makes snap decisions is now activated. Known as the *"Adaptive Unconscious"* by Timothy Wilson, it is a part of the brain that is critical for our survival as human beings. Unless needed for survival, it is on automatic most of the time, ready and waiting to be activated at any moment to warn us of impending danger, launch attacks, pull us into action, and generally determine whether the people and situations we meet are friendly or dangerous. The minute the brain perceives threat: reacts to an unfavorable idea or proposition; meets someone for the very first time; lashes out in anger; or makes decisions under stress for example, it uses this unconscious part of the brain. *Timothy Wilson, "Strangers to Ourselves: Discovering the Adaptive Unconscious". Harvard University press, 2003*

We may well have heard that we take seven to ten seconds to make such critical decisions. In an emergency, seven seconds is an eternity! If you were to notice a tiger lurking in a tree above your head about to pounce, do you imagine that you would contemplate the tiger's beauty for seven seconds until he leaped down on top of you? It would be much more likely that you would size up the situation in an instant, spring into action and rush off, to avoid ending up as a tasty morsel on his dinner menu!

The psychologist Nalini Ambady asked students to rate three ten-second video clips of a teacher, without sound, and asked students to evaluate the teacher's effectiveness. The students were easily able to do this. Ambady cut the clips back to five seconds, and again the students easily rated the teachers' effectiveness. Finally, she cut the clips to **two seconds duration** and amazingly, the snap judgments were just as easily made. She then compared the two-second ratings with the evaluations students made at the end of the whole semester. In essence, the two ratings were the same. Our adaptive

unconscious is a powerful mechanism. It allows us to size up a situation in two seconds, make a decision, and act. *Nalini Ambady, and Robert Rosenthal: "Half a minute Predicting Teacher Evaluations from Thin Slices of Nonverbal Behavior and Physical Attractiveness." Journal of Personality and Social Psychology 64, no. 3, 1993*

This human ability of "short-cut" thinking has been well documented by Malcolm Gladwell in Blink. The term "Thin-slicing" has been coined by John Gottman, a leading authority on human behavior, facial expressions, and rapid cognition. His definition is: "The ability of our unconscious to find patterns in situations and behavior based on very narrow slices of experience." *Malcolm Gladwell, Blink: "The Power of Thinking without Thinking," Little, Brown. 2005.*

A new study by researchers at Carleton University in Ottawa demonstrates that we form opinions in an even shorter timeframe. The study, lead by psychologist, Gitte Lindgaard registered subjects' likes and dislikes from web pages shown in 1/20th of a second.

Evidence such as this illustrating the incredible human capacity for making snap judgments does nothing for our confidence on the dating scene, not to mention its implications in interviews! *Wall Street Journal 2.16.2006: "Moving On," page D4, by Jeffrey Zazlow.*

It is now becoming more obvious why we make such profound, so-called intuitive judgments based on such seemingly superficial evidence as people's dress, facial expressions, and gestures. It is for our own survival of course! It helps us predict threat or danger, gear up for flight or fight and allows us to use old tried and tested strategies to meet people and form relationships. The only problem is that all our information comes from a source of information developed strictly from past experience. It has been coded and encoded along with masses of associations, emotions, sensory data, decisions, and actions, stored in that amazing computer called the cortex.

WHERE DOES ALL THIS FIT FOR IMAGE CONSULTANTS?

If we are human, we all have past histories! The trick is to override that persuasive radio personality stuck in our brain that seems to give us so much free advice. Although we need him or her in emergencies, somehow, he never quite knows when to shut up! I imagine him as the Microsoft paper-clip guy who appears on the screen when I am writing a letter. Adorable when I need him and a pest when I don't.

A recruiter friend of mine once asked me to consult with and advise a young woman who was not doing well in job interviews. When I met the candidate, she was wearing a tight black mini skirt, opaque hose, scuffed high heels, an old navy blue jacket, and rumpled shirt. For the level of employment she was interviewing for, her image needed a revamp; my colleague was relying on me to break the news and give her some pointers.

After the preliminary greetings, I thought I was being my usual friendly self. I asked unthreatening questions about her career path, what kind of positions she was seeking, and general information on which to base my coaching. Every time I asked her about anything the slightest bit personal, I noticed she would stiffen and not divulge any information. I tried to address the image but she was so defensive we got nowhere.

I thought for a minute and decided it was time to clear the air. "Is your image something that's important to you?" I asked with genuine curiosity. "Oh yes, I know I have to improve and I really want to know what I'm doing wrong." She replied. I pressed in again: "Is there anything I've said that has annoyed you?" "No, not at all." She said. "Well...," her voice trailed off and she gazed at the ground. "There is something. Your British accent. When I was in second grade, my teacher was British. She was really nasty to me and I've never been able to stand the accent ever since." There is was, in a nutshell! She could not hear a word I was saying, the associations from the past were so deafening. She went on to describe a particularly unpleasant incident with the teacher and as the story progressed, she got more and more chatty and self-expressed. I held her hand and thanked her for being honest. With that past history out of the way, we were both able to get a great deal more out of the coaching session.

Luckily, if we are willing and able to recognize the baggage, there is no limit to the nonverbal exploration. If you as an image consultant can persuade your clients to explore beyond their limiting self-assessments, or see the point of changing their image, you can continue to help them grow and evolve in appearance, body language, environment, business practices, habits, infrastructure or life-style supports. Granted, some clients are more open than others, their attitudes again rooted in past history.

If we played dress-up as a kid for example, or were in plays or ballet performances or even took part in team sports with uniforms, we were used to changing our image. The minute you were in your soldier costume or your queen's crown you adopted and even *became* that persona; and in your tennis

or baseball outfit, you were ready to play in a different game.

Image consultants say they dress the person the client wants to be. But, who or what is that? The nonverbal language communicates such persuasive messages, that with changes of dress, appearance, language, and nonverbal structures they can be anyone they want to be. Indeed, if you boil it down to the bare bones, we are actually objects wearing things, relating to other objects wearing things! Think of it as a blank canvas on which to design your clients as works of art. This approach is not new. Eliza Doolittle in My Fair Lady was reinvented and passed off as a lady with the help of Professor Higgins, and Scarlet O'Hara who made a gown out of the velvet curtains, raised her desperate status in order to impress the bank manager to borrow money!

As image consultants, you should be constantly looking for ways to make your clients more effective, self-confident, or charismatic. The physical universe is a powerful medium in which to operate. Max Dixon a presentation coach from Seattle and brilliant teacher

calls it "A single, simple do-able thing."
Bring the physical, the structural, the
infrastructure and the body language
from the background to the foreground
and see how it can help your clients put
new structures into practice, and retain
your advice for lasting results.

We have seen how the physical world
and infrastructure play a huge part in our
lives. Resolve to tap into that powerful
language to bring about changes in self-
confidence and self-esteem in your
clients. We can and do transform the
nonverbal world, its language, practices,
habits, dress, and structures, into an ideal
environment for our clients' success. It
is an exciting career!

Chapter 2

SELF IMAGE

"The way in which we think of ourselves has everything to do with how the world sees us"

-Arlene Raven

When we change our clients' physical appearance and body language, do we alter a part of their identity and the way they think about themselves? Image consultants would argue emphatically that we do. Just like the verbal domain, it seems that the nonverbal world has a power of its own. Change it or alter its structure in any way and you change its definition to the world. Simply put, you *are* what you *look like*. You are *what you do* and you are what others *perceive*.

Self-esteem is defined as an individual's overall self-evaluation or sense of self-worth. We tend to appraise our attractiveness as a component of our self worth and many people believe that they are stuck with their lot in life, especially with the way they look. The "You" we are talking about here is the one who has a predictable physical appearance, or at least, the appearance your brain interprets in the mirror on a daily basis.

We now know that the interpretation has been donated to us, care of our memory patterns. Those in turn, have been inherited from our experience: opinions of others, decisions we made from school, family, our culture, college, work, friends, history, geography, television, the media, and advertising.

Kevin Thompson, Ph. D, a professor of psychology at the University of South Florida and author of *"Exacting Beauty: Theory, Assessment and Treatment of Body Image Disturbances"* has done some interesting work on the subjective view of appearance. The internalized view of the way people perceive themselves is a function of our society and culture, perpetuated by advertising and the media. Negative self-image is rampant among girls and young women and often carries over into adulthood. Uncertainty about one's body can lead to lowered self-esteem for both males and females. Researchers have found that women, even more than men, who express dissatisfaction with their weight and body shape actually tend to have lower self-esteem scores than others with a healthier body image. *Turner et al., 1997.*

All this is based on *our reactions* to experiences and to everything that has ever happened to us. We also compare ourselves unfavorably to the examples of beauty set up by the media, often airbrushed, by the way, and constant reminders that we do not look that way.

We as image consultants are constantly bumping up against someone's past history. "I can't wear yellow." "My nose is too long." "I hate my legs and only wear long skirts." "I'm too fat, too thin, too tall, too short, etc." When was the last time you heard someone say, "I'm perfect just as I am?" Take someone shopping, and most people are very clear that they will wear *this* garment but not *that* one! "I can't wear that!" Get their hair cut an inch shorter than they expected, and they get upset. The person in the mirror just does not look like them any more! Where do all these opinions come from? Our past history of course. We cannot alter the past, and unless our clients undergo cosmetic surgery, we cannot alter their physical features. What we can do however, is help them create an exciting and compelling future. If our coaching helps a person invent new and exciting direction, and helps them appreciate how their skills, talents, values, and personality traits contribute to people and the world, I have found with my clients that their self-confidence goes up.

In my experience, self-esteem is enhanced in many ways. If someone has a new job or a new life after an accident or divorce for example, a natural outcome is to value a change of appearance. They now want to present themselves in a way that is consistent with that new direction. Interestingly, I have also found that changes in the nonverbal apparatus (image and body language) also affect the way people view themselves. According to a research study, outlined later, there seems to be a strong link between a new appearance and increased self-esteem. I teach clients and students to walk and stand with a better posture. After a few minutes practice, I ask them how they feel. "Confident!" they yell. "Elegant! Ready to take on the world!"

According to George Wainright, the author of "*Teach Yourself Body Language*," anyone can increase his attractiveness. All we have to do is maintain good eye contact, improve our posture, smile at people we meet and add color to our wardrobe. All of these things can be easily taught to our clients.

How many of us have experienced a new vigor after getting a fresh haircut, or buying a new blazer? Our image is malleable, as is our outlook. We have the tools, tips and techniques for breathing new life into our clients' image, and creating a pleasing appearance with a few simple tricks. When the changes are sustained, not only do we see ourselves in a different light but also the external world begins to acknowledge and reward the transformation! As image consultants, we can use this information with our clients.

The good news is that well-dressed, well-groomed, polished individuals are routinely awarded better salaries, win top jobs, are promoted, and win the approval of their peers.

Sustainability is the critical factor here. High self-esteem develops over time as a function of self-respect. Self-respect is developed in a variety of ways. If you keep your new image going and practice the new skills; set goals to buy a new wardrobe and save the money and then do that; trust yourself to practice the new makeup and keep going to the hair stylist and colorist; create a budget to take on these new assignments; handle disappointments; take failure in its stride and keep on going; separate doing something wrong, as opposed to being a bad or hopeless person, and keep fulfilling your goals, however small, your self esteem will go up.

Tips to Raise Self Esteem

- Think hard and write out a list of what you want.
- Write out your goals and give them a deadline.
- Step into action - do not procrastinate.
- Be accountable to someone else.
- Keep your promises to yourself.
- Walk your Talk
- Practice
- Do what you said you were going to do, zero tolerance!
- Be bold and fall short!
- Celebrate failures and successes.
- Pick yourself up after a fall.
- Identify the lessons you learned.
- Find something to do that contributes to others.

Very soon, people will start reacting to your new image and presence. Studies have shown that they will treat you in a different manner. With constant reinforcement new brain patterns will be established over time as you keep seeing yourself in a different light. All these aspects contribute to the development of a higher self-esteem.

SELF ESTEEM AND RESEARCH

Image consultants have known for many years that they make a difference in a client's outlook and self-confidence. Those of us who have been in the industry a while have written books including case studies on the incredible difference that image has made in their clients' lives. Books such as "*Image Matters*" by Lauren Solomon clearly illustrate that premise. However, little had been researched or documented on the subject until the Association of Image Consultants International (AICI) decided it was time to commission its own research study in 2004.

This image research study showed that image-consulting services give people more than just a "superficial boost." The study established a relationship between image and self-esteem. It demonstrated how simple changes in the physical world could affect the client's ability to

realize and appreciate his or her own self-worth.

The purpose of the in-depth international study was to measure the effectiveness of the work of image consultants and the gain experienced by clients from having participated in consultations. Experts from the marketing department of Central Michigan University designed the study, analyzed results, and conducted the research. This was the first image research study of this nature ever to have been conducted.

Eighty-five clients, representing 18 image consultants in 10 countries, participated in the study. Sixty-six percent completed both the Pre- and Post-service Surveys, while 30 completed two administrations of the Hartman index. The sample consisted of a client profile similar to the one seen on a daily basis by image consultants. The demographics included a high percentage of females (84 percent), aged between 25 and 54 (77 percent), married (53 percent), working full time (66 percent), and residing in the United States (57 percent).

The research study consisted of four components: image influencers, consultation experiences, needs and goal achievements, and difficulty of change. Image consultants volunteered to administer a pre and post survey and measured their clients' needs before and after the services. The surveys were sent in directly by the client and were not translated, influenced or even seen by the consultant. The survey approach allowed for collection of data relating to clients' previous learning about image and personal style, their goal achievement, the perceived value of the consultation, their satisfaction with the consultation, 42 measures of their needs in the areas of appearance, self- image, personal and professional development, and relevant demographic information.

In addition, self-esteem measures were obtained using the Hartman Self Esteem Index® in a pre- and post- service setting, administered via e-mail (or paper and pencil, if necessary). Self-esteem was defined as the client's ability to realize and appreciate his or her own self-worth.

Of the clients completing a pre- and a post- Hartman Self Esteem Index®, 63 percent experienced gains in their self-esteem scores, sometimes by an appreciable amount.

In those clients whose self-esteem indexes remained the same, in all cases the completion of both initial and final Hartman Index occurred on the same day. It is possible to draw some conclusions from these level results. First, it was likely that not enough learning had taken place to effect changes with these clients; not enough time had elapsed for the clients to internalize their learning, and finally perhaps the consultation itself did not address issues of self-esteem for the client.

However, the average summary score on the index, across all matched pairs, increased from 6.92 prior to consultation to 7.28 following consultation, ten percent, (on a 0-10 scale). This increase is significant, from both a practical and a statistical sense.

The study reports: "It is truthful to state that clients' self-esteem, as measured by the Hartman Self Esteem Index®, was higher following the consultations than before. It is accurate to say that these results were overwhelmingly positive."

Other components evaluated in the Index that showed appreciable changes were self-assessment, self-improvement, self-management, and internal self-esteem.

IMAGE INFLUENCERS:

Clients learned about image and personal style from a variety of sources, but most often from their parents and peers. Forty percent had received no formal or informal teaching about their image or personal style. Thirty-eight percent indicated that their teaching was indirect, 22% had learned through makeup demonstrations, looking at magazines and shopping with friends. Eighteen percent learned through criticism. They learned about image consulting through referrals more than other methods.

CONSULTATION EXPERIENCES:

In every single case, clients were extremely satisfied with their consultation experience, giving extremely high ratings to their image consultants in all areas queried. In addition, their perception of the value of the sessions to them, personally, was extremely high. In 100% of consultations both their satisfaction and value ratings averaged between four and five on a one-to-five scale. Interestingly, the clients outside the US were even more satisfied with results than US clients were.

NEEDS AND GOAL ACHIEVEMENT:

In all client consultations, there were significant differences between clients' pre-service and post-service ratings of their needs. Following the consultation sessions, clients perceived their needs to be lower and in all cases clients believed strongly that they had achieved their goals. Clients who were over 35, married, working full time and living in the US had greater goal achievement scores in the area of self-confidence, but in all cases clients perceived their goals had been met, especially related to Appearance:

- Proper clothing fit,
- What type of clothing suits me?
- What colors suit me?
- How do I look up to date?
- I want a new direction for my image.

In Self-Image the greatest item of change was, "I need a new direction for my image." However all items showed significant positive changes in the post service results.

> *On the personal and professional development areas, the study comments: "The evidence shows that the image consulting sessions provided to these clients were resoundingly successful at reducing clients' perceived needs."*

DIFFICULTY OF CHANGE

Questions on personal change were included in the study because image consultants recognize that positive results often depend on the amount of physical, mental, or emotional personal change the client is willing to make.

Image changes can be difficult and even frightening to some people. A surprising result of this study showed that personal change was perceived to be easier after the sessions. The goal of professional development was perceived as requiring the easiest change but even in the more challenging areas of self-image, self-confidence and self-esteem, personal change was deemed easier after the consultations than before. Interestingly, females over 35 perceived that self-confidence would be easier to change than younger women or males.

The ease of change reported is significant, because part of the work of image consultants is to empower and help people change, give people the permission to change, provide support and to facilitate the process through education, tips and techniques.

STUDY CONCLUSIONS

The information gathered from this study will be valuable on many counts. It validates that the work of image consultants is important not only on a superficial level but also demonstrates a relationship between a client's image and her ability to realize and appreciate his or her own self-worth. Image services also have a significant impact on personal and professional development skills that relate to the areas people deem most important in life: self-confidence, career, promotion, work performance and interpersonal relationships. The bulk of our clients are female in the 18-64 age range, married or single and working full time. This is a very wide market and becoming broader as more people learn about image consulting.

It is now possible to state that the study has established a relationship between image, or "outside" and the "inside" or human element. This will become the characteristic that most differentiates image consulting as the industry grows in the future.

The study will help the public realize that image consultants do not have to perform extreme makeovers or work with their clients for years to impact their self-confidence. The average number of sessions in this sample was 2.18 ranging from 1 to 12 hours maximum. Image consulting makes a big difference in a small amount of time!

APPEARANCE IS KEY TO SUCCESS

Over the years, several studies have shown the importance of physical appearance as a determining factor for how the world relates to us. Although these studies were based on a U.S. target audience, in my experience, having lived in four countries and worked in eight different countries, these results demonstrate a human propensity in all cultures to admire and emulate pleasing proportions and colors; good teeth, skin, hair and eyes and self confidence among our peers. This of course is not only human! Many studies of animal behavior have demonstrated similar results.

The interesting thing in these instances is that varieties of positive traits quite unrelated to image were attributed to the attractive individuals. In many studies, self-confidence, even more than physical beauty plays a huge part in the traits people find attractive in each other.

In their classic study of judgmental bias, '*What is beautiful is good*', Dion, Berscheid and Walster (1972) asked subjects to choose which personality traits applied to pictures of attractive and unattractive people. Their results showed that traits that are more positive were attributed to the attractive individuals, as compared to the less attractive individuals. This bias, or halo effect, was obtained consistently over a wide range of rated traits and personal qualities. Many further studies have repeated these findings, showing this bias as well. For example in studies done by Kalick, 1988; Saladin, Saper, & Breen, 1988;

Walster, Aronson, Abrahams, & Rottman, 1966, subjects consistently indicated their belief that people that are more attractive possess superior personal qualities.

Other studies indicating the power of physical appearance include a 1981 study by Worsley that indicated a negative interpretation of obesity in the workplace. The study showed that men and women who are obese are considered to have personalities that set them at a disadvantage in the workplace. Obese men were considered lazy and lacking willpower.

When it comes to the workplace, most people find that physical attractiveness is important. A majority of people studied believed that clothing, hair, and makeup are particularly important aspects for a woman to consider for the sake of her job and career. In studies, nearly seven in ten (69%) considered that clothing, hair and makeup were very or extremely important for a woman to make a good impression on the job. Only seven percent of those studied did not consider it at all important.

In fact, a woman's image was deemed even more significant when it came to influencing certain aspects of her future performance on the job.

- 84% believe a woman's appearance affects whether she is asked to represent her company at outside meetings
- 76% believe it affects whether she is taken seriously
- 74% believe it affects whether she is asked to participate in meetings with upper management
- 74% consider it affects whether she is well regarded by colleagues and supervisors
- 67% believe a well groomed woman will be given new challenges, responsibilities, and opportunities
- 64% believe that she will be considered for a raise or promotion

It might be expected in the image conscious business world that people would consider image important to their success and influence on coworkers, bosses, and associates. However, it is more surprising that they believe that their appearance actually affects the way in which they perform their jobs. Nevertheless, a solid percentage of people reported that they consider that a woman's appearance affects her confidence in her ability to perform her job. Nearly half (46%) considered that clothes, hair and makeup affect a woman's confidence in her ability to perform her job well followed by one-third (32%) who believed it is somewhat true. Image consultants have known this anecdotally of course for years, but it was not until the AICI 2004 Research Study that we had more solid evidence to draw a relationship between self-confidence, self-respect, self-esteem, and image. Further evidence suggests that a woman's appearance at work affects her ability to perform her job well. More than half (59%) considered that appearance is a factor, while 36%

believe appearance does not affect work abilities and performance.

GOOD LOOKS AND THE PAY SCALE

When it comes to earnings, it seems that certain aspects of appearance count. A University of Florida study found that there was a correlation between good looks and earning potential: tall people make more money! A business research team at the University of North Carolina at Chapel Hill analyzed the results of four large-scale studies in the US and Britain. The study examined personal and professional details of thousands of participants from childhood to adulthood.

> *Each inch in height added about $789 per year in pay.*

Supervisors correlated people's height with greater effectiveness on the job, and the relationship between height and earnings in sales and management was particularly noticeable.

An article in the Financial Times October 29, 2003, quotes a study proving the correlation between good looks and earning potential. Plain people earn 5% to 10% less than people of average looks who earn 3% to 8% less than good-looking people do. Studies done by Professor Daniel Hamermesh at the University of Texas, Jeff Biddle of Michigan University and a London Guildhall University Study of 11,000 33-year olds all concur on this result. Interestingly, self-confidence, even more than physical beauty plays a huge part in the traits people find attractive in each other. Surprisingly, the penalty for being plain was greater for men than women. Men who ranked with below average looks were paid 10% less than their handsome peers were. Very attractive women were paid 4% more.

"Why Beautiful People will be Handsomely Rewarded," Michael Skapinker

The fact remains, that despite resounding evidence that image will have an affect on their success, business people are not taking advantage of our services. A Sales & Marketing Management Magazine article, *"The Power Look is Back"* reports that few sales and marketing managers have sought professional help to improve their look. Only 11% of respondents to an S&MM/Equation Research Survey have hired image consultants to work with their sales force, 12% have used one for themselves, and among those who did, 87% said it made an impact on their success.

Chapter 3

HOW TO MAKE A DIFFERENCE WITH YOUR CLIENTS

In my experience, the people who are attracted to image consulting are caring, compassionate human beings. There is not one person I have trained who does not have an ardent desire to help people feel better about themselves, be more confident, find their potential, develop their best self, and create an external presence to represent that. As a breed, our strongly developed critical capacities, training, and attention to detail can tell us in a twinkling of an eye what is wrong with someone's image and how to fix it. While the general female public is agonizing over large thighs, we can make her look like a toothpick in twenty seconds with a few artful tips. That's the good news!

The bad news is that those capacities are hard to shut off when not needed. Have you noticed that your thoughts do not take a break? At the beginning of my career I was really an annoying companion. I would put my image-correcting thoughts on loudspeaker and constantly sounded very critical and nasty to the people around me, particularly my family. Then I had an epiphany! I realized with a jolt that all my thoughts were actually condemning people who did not have a great image. (or great in my opinion, that is!) I could see that in my mind, something was inherently *wrong* with them and they needed to be set straight.

Not a powerful platform from which to empower people to transform their own image! I wondered why people would twitch nervously and fiddle with their hair and collar every time I came near, and breathe a sigh of relief if I gave them a compliment. "Oh good, today I passed." Very soon, my family just rolled their eyes and stopped listening to a word I said.

Since then, I have thought of image as a language that you learn or do not learn in school. Some of us learned French, others did not. Not knowing French does not make you a bad person. It was even easier for me to think in terms of Mandarin. I was never taught Mandarin and cannot even decipher the alphabet or guess at the words. I would be completely lost in China, but I am still not a despicable person!

From that perspective, I grew by leaps and bounds, more as an image coach, than a consultant. I provided structures and stepping stones, models and exercises, role-play and formats, processes and frameworks! There was no end to the ways in which I could whittle out people's magnificent version of themselves. Making a difference was more about my ability to walk in the shoes of my clients, trainees and seminar participants; presenting and guiding choices; rather than inflicting a point of view. In short, I learned the power of service. I was more inspired to look now at their results short and long-term; to watch as more client and participant evaluations said, "I was made to think," and "I was spurred on to find out more." I stood for growth and development *in the world*, and we are all included in that. It was no longer about me!

George Bernard Shaw said it best:

"This is the true joy of life, the being used for a purpose recognized by yourself as being a mighty one: the being a force of nature instead of a feverish, selfish little clod of ailments and grievances complaining that the world will not devote itself to making you happy. I am of the opinion that my life belongs to the whole community, and as long as I live it is my privilege to do for it whatever I can. I want to be thoroughly used up when I die, for the more I create the more I live. I rejoice in life for its own sake. Life is no brief candle to me. It is a sort of splendid torch which I have got hold of for the moment, and I want to make it burn as brightly as possible before handing it on to future generations."

George Bernard Shaw

The mindset that now prevailed was that nothing is wrong! I do not have to "fix" you. Instead, I have a set of tools to pass on if you choose to take them, and it is your choice. I do not have to impose my (albeit fantastic!) taste on you. I can now come to terms with the fact that I have critiqued you and corrected you in my mind in two seconds flat. With that over, I can put my critical powers to rest and really get to know you. What freedom! I am able to listen to and appreciate you for the *person* you are, what you *stand for,* and where you want to grow and develop yourself. The rest is just a matter of teaching you the language and skills should you ask for them.

FROM INSPIRATION TO ACTION

As you go about building your image consulting business, you will begin to realize that the increased success you are seeking depends on the success of your clients. Hone your listening skills for not only where they can grow, but also where you can strengthen your practices. Your growth will foster your clients' growth exponentially.

How many of us long to inspire our clients, friends and family; press them to taste the opportunities of an enhanced image, inject them with a renewed sense of self confidence and motivate them to a higher level of inspired action?

Inspiration: The dictionary defines it as: *Stimulation of the faculties to a high level of feeling or activity.* The word comes from the Latin *inspirare,* to breathe life into!

How do we inspire our clients to change their appearance and behavior and how do we persuade potential clients to hire us? I am of the mind that inspiration itself happens in the hearts and minds of each individual listener as they prompt themselves to think in a new direction. Action is a completely different thing all together, yet we sometimes confuse the two.

In Martin Luther King's speech, we can all hear ourselves in his words and be moved:

> *I have a dream today! With this faith, we will be able to hew out of the mountain of despair a stone of hope. With this faith, we will be able to transform the jangling discords of our nation into a beautiful symphony of brotherhood. With this faith we will be able to work together, to pray together, to struggle together, to go to jail together, to stand up for freedom together, knowing that we will be free one day.*
> *I have a dream that my four little children will one day live in a nation where they will not be judged by the color of their skin but by the content of their character.*
>
> Martin Luther King Jr.

If people can hear themselves, in your underlying message, and what you are saying, they will be stimulated. If they can identify with the words or deeds and say, "I want that" or "I can do that or "That sounds like me," or "I can say that!" they are inspired. Unlike the store or boutique associate, our role as consultants is to nudge people to think differently about themselves; give them permission to look, act, speak, and behave at a higher level. Inspiration happens when our words are now embedded in the mind of our clients and they can own them for themselves.

When Nelson Mandela delivered these words it was a shot that echoed around the world. We could all hear ourselves in the message:

> *Our deepest fear is not that we are inadequate. Our deepest fear is that we are powerful beyond measure. It is our light not our darkness that most frightens us. We ask ourselves, "Who am I to be brilliant, gorgeous, talented, and fabulous?"*
>
> *Actually, who are you NOT to be? You are a child of God. Your playing small does not serve the world. There is nothing enlightened about shrinking so that others will not feel insecure around you.*
>
> *We were born to make manifest the glory of God that is within us. It is not just in some of us. It is in everyone, and, as we let our light shine, we unconsciously give other people permission to do the same. As we are liberated from our own fear, our presence automatically liberates others.*
>
> *Nelson Mandela quoting Marianne Williamson in his 1994 Inaugural speech.*

So What Happens Between Inspiration And Action?

Unfortunately, inspiration has a very short shelf life! For example, when you are selling your services, your potential clients can be visibly inspired at the time, yet when you call them back a day or two later their enthusiasm has fallen off dramatically. What happened? Real-life comes up like a tsunami wave hitting us in the face, and inspiration goes down the tubes. What was missing in your conversation was the HOW. We sense that someone is inspired but we do not always build the bridge to action.

It is hard not to get frustrated when people do not immediately rush into action just because they had a breakthrough in thinking! Actually, thinking and taking action involve very different thought processes. If inspiration is breathing life into the thoughts, then the next step is to breathe life into the body to make a move! The important next step for us is to help the client or potential client work out circumstances that are sufficiently favorable to make it happen. If we leave out this piece in the sales presentation, we risk losing the sale; if left out in the consultation, the client may not take our advice all the way.

Take the sales presentation for example. In sales, a few questions will sometimes handle it such as, "What do you need to make this happen?" "What's our next move?" "Is there anything you see that might prevent our moving forward?" At other times, you may have to address some uncomfortable issues, do some handholding, or give multiple suggestions and examples of how others handled similar situations. Very gently, you are helping to build a feasible bridge to the action plan. If they are not able to overcome roadblocks with your help, the sale might falter and die on the vine. To move your clients or groups to the next phase of their transformation the same process needs to take place. Some people will be ready to spring into action. Others will procrastinate until you despair that nothing will ever change. These people need a lot of bridge building until it is safe to venture out. Change can be scary.

Think of the image consultation as another example. If our mission in life is to empower people, we certainly need a way to get through to them and help

them over the roadblocks. There may be things to work out such as time or money, where to shop, the type of clothes to buy, what capsule to start with or how to attack the closet. Do not invalidate yourself if you don't get the results you are seeking from your client right away. Remember, this is a process. If I am shopping for a female client, I frequently go through all the clothes she likes and work out what to buy the first time we shop, and what to leave until next time. You may think, "Surely that's part of our job?", but you will be surprised how often we leave out the customer service aspect.

The next time someone is inspired or excited by your words and wants to buy your services or transform their image, remember that the road from inspiration to action is not a straight line. There may be a few detours along the way. Here is a model to take someone from Inspiration to Action:

- *Build relationship*
- *Build trust*
- *Build inspiration*
- *Build the bridge*
- *Build a watertight action plan*

Look to see if even one of those was missing or weak last time a sale went south or a client crept back to his comfort zone!

CLOTHING

As we have discovered, image consultants deal for the most part with the physical world and indeed, that is what makes our coaching so effective. We upgrade clients' style and quality, and choose clothes that they would not necessarily choose for themselves.

When I shop for clients, it is exciting and enlightening. In every case, with every one of the clients there is a defining moment when each sees him or herself differently in the mirror for the first time. In that moment, their experience of themselves changes and it is visible in their bodies. They straighten up, stop talking, stare at themselves in amazement, and see themselves in a new light, literally as a new person. Their demeanor becomes more confident, their faces clear and they gasp at the sight of themselves. I know then that we need to nail that outfit down and ask the tailor to come. Carpe Diem! They might get scared and have a change of heart.

One client even shed a tear to see herself so slim, alluring, and elegant. Another male client became a transformed human being! He dropped his apologetic air and started to take command of situations. He wrote a classified advertisement for the personals, and described himself as an attractive, lovable man he hardly recognized but could now become. A formerly rather timid client wore her new clothes to work and was immediately overwhelmed with compliments. "They are actually starting to ask my opinion about things," she said. None of these people had liposuction or cosmetic surgery, been on a diet, or sat in a therapist's office, but the change was just as dramatic!

As amazing as it may seem to some, the physical communication of clothing is so powerful it can transform a person's outlook. As image consultants, we all know that self-confidence is sometimes just a new outfit away!

LANGUAGE

Since image consultants deal with the physical world, the type of language we use with our clients plays an important role. Judging from the success of New Year's Resolutions, many people have a hard time reaching their goals. After we have declared, "This time, I'm going to do it," we live in the world of "thinking about it and hoping and trying," and somehow, it never happens. We have a weak relationship to the available infrastructure and how it can help us achieve our goals. In this case, infrastructure represents the physical environment that we can harness to support our goals.

Change *your* language with your clients. Rather than just making suggestions, recommendations and leaving it up to your clients, ask for goals and concentrate on physical changes. Ask "By when will you do that?" Then follow up. Do not leave it to chance, and you will bring about more rapid transformations. At that point, your approach needs to be more coaching than consulting. For example, if they want to lose weight they have to PLAN the weekly meals on a sheet of paper not in their heads; SHOP for a different type of food and get rid of the rest in their fridge and cupboards; actually SET an appointment in their day timer with their trainer or gym, arrange their calendar and the people around them to support them, BUY workout shoes and GO to the gym.

STRESS

Become a stress-o-meter for your clients. Being stressed out is bad for the image! It makes you look disorganized, scatter-brained, and uncaring. It also takes its toll on your face and body. Wherever your clients have stress in their lives, ensure that they make "on the court" changes in infrastructure so their actions immediately change on a daily basis. Do not leave it to descriptive language that swims around in their head. Time is a huge stressor for many people. What physical alterations can they make in their day so their mind is more relaxed and their image more self-assured? A realistic written plan first springs to mind. Then following it every day! Physically saying: "No, not now, but by x time", is a muscle we all need to strengthen. Exercise and walks can all be planned into a well-organized daily

praise mones by Laurette Willis

regime. For instance, Yoga is a wonderful way to introduce a form of meditation into your life that clears your thoughts. You can often detect changes of mindset, feelings of well-being and even a calmer frame of mind after physical activity, thanks largely to the power of those endorphins!

One simple thing I did personally to rid myself of driving stress was to drive on the surface roads, and avoid the interstates or access roads. I allowed more time, took longer, met less traffic, planned my routes through beautiful tree lined neighborhoods, listened to tapes and the radio, and arrived refreshed.

ENERGY

Have you noticed that often your energy level has very little to do with the hours of sleep you had? Of course, we cannot go days on end with inadequate sleep, but an amazing human phenomenon is that we can be physically tired and still have an animated, fun conversation with someone or engage in something that fascinates us and hardly feel tired at all. Why did all that exhaustion suddenly slip away?

Our energy actually comes from an infinite source; a well that never runs dry and is always available to us. To tap into it you have to be willing to look back at your past experiences and do some preparation before you begin to create something new. By doing this as a regular practice, you can easily recharge your batteries whenever you are feeling exhausted, (if you know the cause is not chronic lack of sleep). It works like a tonic!

Energy level has everything to do with what you have accomplished and what you have completed. If you are constantly stressed and feeling you will never catch up, no amount of creating new projects will ever feel fulfilling. Why? Because, like icing on a mud pie they will be plastered on top of everything that was incomplete from the past. The things you did not do, the weight you did not lose, the client you did not get, the work you did not finish, the conversations you never had or never brought to a satisfactory result, and the failures you dwell on like a recurring bad dream will all be there just below the surface whenever you begin to create! A new idea has a shelf life of about three hours. After that, the old thoughts, resignation, cynicism, and "yes-buts" start to creep back in.

COMPLETION

First, it is important to draw a distinction between finishing something and completing something. Finishing is to *come* to an end, as in finishing a book. You do not talk about completing a book unless you are the author! Completion on the other hand is to make whole, to *bring* to an end, *although you might not have necessarily finished anything.* Even though nothing is finished you have the ability to declare things whole and complete. For example, you can be in the middle of a project, yet every evening you can stop everything and *declare* that the day is complete. You can do the tasks you need to do to be able to leave the project mid-stream, clear away the mess on your desk, and leave it for the night.

"The quality or state of being complete," is also the definition of integrity. You can restore your integrity and bring anything from the past whole-heartedly to an end with a flourish, by acknowledging your failures, your disappointments, unfulfilled expectations, achievements, accomplishments, and what you did and did not do, and put it all to rest.

You can do this alone but it is best to do it with a buddy, a coach, a spouse, or a colleague and be sure not to get into any arguments over any of it. All you are going to do is to write down and acknowledge some facts. The trick is to embrace and *own* your human frailties! Declare yourself complete with each item. You cannot alter the past. Do not beat yourself up. Here is the test. If you do this, you will no longer dwell on the things on your list. As you empty your mind, peace and energy will flood in. If you are still incomplete, you will keep thinking about it.

Before any new project starts, write down the answers to the questions on the next page. If you cannot think of anything for one question, move on to the next.

What did you not do that you said you would do?

_____

_____

_____

To whom do you still need to communicate something?

_____

_____

_____

What regrets do you have?

_____

_____

_____

What resentments do you have?

_____

_____

_____

What disappointments do you have?

_____

_____

_____

What unfinished business do you have?

_____

_____

_____

What did you expect that did not come to pass?

_____

_____

_____

What failures did you have?

_____

_____

_____

What did you accomplish?

_____

_____

_____

What are you proud of?

_____

_____

_____

What leaps forward did you take?

_____

_____

_____

What new skills did you develop?

_____

_____

_____

What results did you achieve?

_____

_____

_____

How did you contribute to others?

_____

_____

_____

Who in your family grew and developed?

_____

_____

Who of your clients grew and developed?

_____

_____

_____

Now, share your lists with a partner and have a good laugh, a good cry and shred, burn or destroy both lists. If you still need to communicate with some people, put their name and number in your day timer and call them as soon as possible. Other great energizing activities are to file your papers, create filing systems not piling systems, organize and tidy closets and cupboards, make beds, do a closet purge for yourself, get your bank account straight, throw away junk, clean the car, get the garden in shape for the winter and complete anything else that is on your mind.

TIME MANAGEMENT

An easy way to reduce stress for your clients is to help them organize their day so there is enough time for emergencies. They should leave enough time for traffic jams, dressing calamities, make-up snafus, breakdowns, returning calls, doing errands and E-mail. E-mail, TV and the internet have become major time wasters. Ask them to work out on paper how much of their day is spent in non-essential activities and how much time they can create just by taking conscious control of their day by turning off the TV, doing E-mail at certain times and leaving internet browsing until after hours.

PERSONAL ORGANIZATION SYSTEMS

We are in the business of altering how a person thinks of him or herself. If we are successful, the world will also perceive your client as transformed. Go to work on your client's infrastructure. The best way to ensure that image changes last longer than your visit is to include actual organization of their closet, wardrobe, personal space, and drawers as part of

your consultations. When you leave they should be able to find anything in five seconds! Can they mix and match their clothes if the garments are in two different closets, under the bed or in a drawer in the basement? I once did a wardrobe assessment for a man who met me outside his storage unit in an industrial part of town. He had all his best clothes in storage and had to drive several miles to dress for an interview or a dressy occasion. Not a good strategy for effective dressing, not to mention the 100-degree (40'C) heat that was cooking his clothes every day!

PROFESSIONAL ORGANIZATION SYSTEMS

Your working spaces speak volumes! Aim to have an office where you can access anything in five seconds.

- Have everything under one subject in one, not several places.
- When you are filing, make one action with one piece of paper one time.
- Do not move things from place to place or shuffle papers into more piles. It's a waste of time!
- Find a place for everything and put everything in its place. Your mother was correct!
- File different subjects under different color files.
- File every morning or when your mind is sharp. The activity will go much faster.

WORKING WITH WOMEN

To a woman clothes are expressions of her life in all its colors. On the whole women enjoy variety. Clothes represent all her moods, aspirations, and dreams; they tell stories and reflect the many dimensions of her personality. If she wants to demonstrate another aspect of her personality, she has only to alter her hair and makeup and change her style. Every garment hanging in her closet tells a tale. Find out from your client whether those tales are the ones she wants the world to know. Is her past still hanging around in her closet? Perhaps it needs to be shown the door and be replaced by a new and exciting future. An overhaul of her wardrobe and closet could do wonders for her morale and free her from the constraints of past history. Dress her for the future she intends to have and she might be pleasantly surprised at what happens to her.

Does the whole closet have a "Wardrobe Wizard" or a mastermind behind the sets of clothes hanging there? A well-developed wardrobe will contain three types of purchases. First good quality garments such as coats, raincoats and eveningwear, which are investments she should make for the long term. Next, she will have some outfits. These are clothes that are always worn together, such as suit skirts and jackets that cannot be split and look odd paired with anything else. Finally she will have the clothes that have versatility and can be mixed and matched in capsules or groups. These groups would be arranged in colors that go together with the same type of fabric, color scheme, style, and character. They tell the same story.

If she only buys outfits and investment pieces, it may be time to branch out and have some more fun with her clothes. This is where you come in. You can go through the wardrobe and take out the garments that no longer represent her. You will teach her to shop in a new and more efficient way and buy a collection of clothes that mix and match and work to create a new image! For instance, the clothes in a capsule should all travel beautifully together and require only one pair of shoes, so that she has already cut down on her packing problems right there!

To most women, high fashion is for tall leggy, thin models, but not for them. Help your clients adapt fashion so they feel current, stylish, and pulled together, but not a victim to fashion. A style catches on because the climate is right for a change and we are ready for something new. The vast majority of women will usually buy something when their eye has become accustomed to the new style.

FADS

These are the clothes that have exaggerated lines, unusual fabric combinations, and experimental style mixes. They flout convention at all costs and are intended for a very young market. Chunky platform shoes, embroidered jeans, scarf blouses that tie with strings at the back, tattoos and body piercing, bare midriffs, blue and lime green nail polish are all examples of fad fashion that will go out before you are ready for your next hair cut!

TRENDS

These clothes have adopted some fashion features such as the current skirt length or jacket shape. The lines and silhouettes of the clothes come from high fashion or fad fashion but have been modified to appeal to a wider market. Stretch fabrics and blends replaced 100% natural fabrics; short jackets replaced medium, replaced long; cropped pants replaced long, straight replaced pleated, and low rise replaced waisted.

The trend look usually contains elements of the original fashion look but becomes modified and less exaggerated in its interpretation. For example shoulder pads, oversized boyfriend jackets and long skirts favored throughout the eighties were replaced by short straight skirts, straight front pants, lean tailored and fitted jackets, and small shoulder pads for the last years of the nineties. The current tailored clothes have little or no shoulder pads and minimal construction. These narrow styles, stripped of their interfacing and padding have already lasted as trends for a few years and are well on their way to becoming classics.

CLASSICS

Blazers, straight or pleated skirts, sheath dresses, bob hairstyles, pump shoes, pearls, and trench coats have been around long enough to stand the test of time. Classics have no exaggerated features, follow the form of the body, and are generally in hardwearing fabrics, which will last long after you have tired of them. A classic will last about eight to ten years and will be worn by a very wide public. Examples of trends that have become recent classics are animal prints, fitted jackets, straight leg pants, shirts, knitted twin sets, layered and razor-cut hairstyles, and shorter pants.

TREND-CLASSIC

If your client is a businesswoman, she needs to project an image of professionalism. She also needs to look updated and modern. You would do best to buy Trend or Trend-Classic garments for her that have been around long enough not to look faddish yet give her an image of being fashionable and current. If she insists on wearing all classics she runs the risk of looking old fashioned and stodgy! If she wears all

the latest fad fashions (even in fashion industries) she will appear to be at the whim of fashion, uncertain of her style and unsure of the values she stands for. Trend or Trend -Classic styles will stand the test of time and are worth buying in good quality fabrics as an investment for the future.

HAIR

Changes in hairstyle are even more radical alterations in infrastructure, since after all, that thatch on the top of her head is part of her identity from a very young age.

Change that, and suddenly her self-image has altered. Our hair may be just an object to some people, but to most of us it is a significant part of our representation to the world. If a woman is ready to give up her long hair, my hairstylist will seize the moment and cut a chunk off straight across the back and give it to her, before styling the rest. He calls it a "rite of passage."

The most important change you can make to your client's image is the hairstyle. It can make or break the new outfits. A new do can make even old clothes seem updated.

MAKEUP

Makeup is another physical change that alters the way we realize our self-image. When the economy goes south, the sale of makeup goes up. The effect on women goes way beyond a little paint on the face. One of my clients told me I changed her life by outlining her tiny lips with a pencil and giving her a Cupid's Bow! She could not believe how it made a difference to her self-confidence and her look. Eventually she got a permanent lip line. If you do not do the makeup yourself for your clients, make sure you have a makeup artist as a resource. It will make a huge difference to your clients' self-image, however lightly applied.

THE ART AND SCIENCE OF WORKING WITH MALE CLIENTS

To most men fabric, fit, styles, pattern, color, texture, coordination, and knowing the right accessories are all a mystery. They are aware that they must somehow clothe their bodies but of even greater importance are three things. First, the clothes must feel comfortable and the pathway to assembling the pieces must be easy and quick. The underlying concepts must follow a system of guidelines or rules that appeal to men. As a consultant, your operating procedure and advice when working with male clients must therefore follow these three principles:

- Simplicity
- Comfort
- Logic

Men are largely traditionalists. Most men do not crave to know the details of color; they simply want to know what suits them and what does not. They want to know the rules of coordination, the correct pant, jacket and sleeve length, and which tie can be matched with which jacket, pants and shirt. They may also be interested in improving the shape of their body with clothes.

Your advice should be delivered in the form of checklists, guidelines, rules, and rationale. Do not be oblique or unclear in your critiques. Tell them what not to wear and what to wear for their body type, coloring, industry and the professional level to which they aspire. Make it easy, clear, and logical.

Of extreme importance to a man are his status, hierarchy, and power. Men understand immediately that human beings evaluate each other; they do it all the time. However it may be news to them that clothes play such an important part in that evaluation process. The concept of projecting a message consistent with his skills, talents and vision then becomes very relevant to a man who is upwardly mobile, interviewing or on the dating scene. If he understands that a consistent appearance and presence will help him get a job, funding for a company, a loan, a promotion, or a date, he will be more likely to listen to you! He can then see that if people respond favorably to his image every time they see him, they will also build a trust level in his performance in other areas.

An inconsistent image or mixed messages, on the other hand could leave his business associates unsure of his performance level, aspirations and goals in life. An advisor I work with was counseling a young man who was seeking seed capital. I critiqued the aspiring entrepreneur in a workshop. He was wearing a soiled, creased shirt, baggy chinos, a full beard, and hair stretching down his back. The advice he received from his counselor was quite clear. "Unless your name is Gates, they don't give money to guys with pony-tails!" He immediately cut his hair, shaved his facial hair and wore a crisp shirt, jacket and tie. Within weeks, he was funded.

SECRETS OF MEN'S SHOES

It is no secret to us that men love comfort in their clothes. The same goes for their shoes. You may also wonder why men's shoes cost so much, but there are many reasons for the high price.

For example, many Italian shoe manufacturers saturate the virgin leather in oil for at least one month and then compress the leather to a third of its thickness. With cheaper shoes, they will split the leather to make it thinner but it will end up stiff, hard, and uncomfortable.

The most expensive shoes are kept on the shoemaker's last for at least a week to mold the shape, a method that also keeps the shoe as soft as glove leather. Expensive and hand crafted shoes use top-grade leather with no scars or nicks such as the finest calf or woven leathers to maintain the comfort.

Dying the leather is also quite an art. The Analin dyed method employed by craftsmen and designers such as Ferragamo allows the color to penetrate all the way through the leather and keeps it soft. Check the shoe to see if the leather is one color on top and another on the underside. Cheaper shoes are made of split leather, sanded down, and sprayed.

However, you can get comfort even if the shoes do not need a second mortgage! Take, for example, Johnston and Murphy. Since 1852 they have prided themselves on making the best men's ready to wear shoes. They have devised a trampoline cushioning system in some of their shoes where they employ layers and layers of foam-like material so that it feels like you are walking on air. And you are!

They have also made an "airport friendly" shoe that contains no metal and will not set off any detectors at the airport. The shoe has a fiberglass shank instead of steel, which is great when every second counts to catch that flight. The gel insert in some of their shoes has 100% memory for the foot created by a unique eggshell design and is anti-odor, anti-fungal, and anti-bacterial.

J&M will also welcome back the shabbiest of shoes for a spiffy revamp and a total refurbish so they give their shoes a lifetime guarantee.

FITTING A MAN'S SHIRT

> *Measure the neck and add 3/4"*
> *To measure the arm, place the tape on the large vertebrae under the neck in between the shoulders. Run it around the elbow to 1" below the wrist bone.*
> *Move the cuff button for a snug fit around the wrist.*
> *The cuff should show ¼" beyond the coat sleeve.*
> *Dress shirt shoulders should extend no more than ¼" off the shoulders. Casual shirts can extend over the shoulders for a more relaxed fit.*
> *Allow for shrinkage: the dress shirt should have at least 1" of room on either side of the body.*

DRESSING YOUNG PEOPLE

"I'm in my mid thirties and look eighteen.
Please can you help me?"

This is a common cry of help from a new section of the population: young executives! In the past, the majority of my clients and the ones sent to me by large organizations have been in their forties and fifties. This is no longer the case as young people are being promoted to executive and management positions much earlier than in previous decades. Companies and entrepreneurial ventures are snatching up bright young things with education, technical expertise, and confidence and launching them on fast-track careers. Highly capable, intelligent, and knowledgeable people ask for image consulting, all with the same concern. They know their stuff but they look or dress so young nobody is taking them seriously, least of all the people they may manage, who might be as old as their parents.

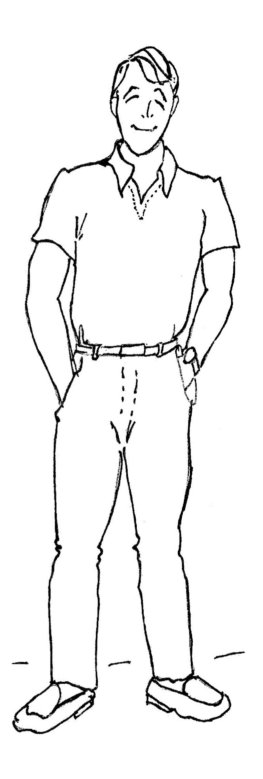

Young people would also die rather than dress like their parents' generation. They like their clothes tighter (or looser), their hair longer and their fashions more exaggerated. They are willing to show more skin and have their hair flowing. The message they are sending is one of youth and inexperience and they wonder why nobody takes them seriously!

One young woman of twenty-eight had to oversee a multi-million dollar advertising budget and was working with experienced advertising people. She wore very tight fitting pantsuits, low-cut stretch tops, and thigh-high skirts and refused to cut her shoulder-blade length hair. Although she was capable of doing the job, she was constantly being asked by clients if they could speak to her manager. She would reply through clenched teeth: I am the manager!" We worked with her over a period of a few months and gradually she realized that she could be sexy outside of work and attractive at work. Well fitting clothes were an asset to her and demonstrated professionalism. Her hair could still be gorgeous when shorter, cut to the shoulders, or worn up, and cleavages

were distracting to both men and women in the business world. She changed her appearance to become an attractive addition to the company and got the reputation of someone with beauty and brains.

Three other young men were opening new divisions and had to hire older employees; yet another at the grand old age of thirty-one was about to become the CEO of a consulting firm. He had to procure funding from older potential investors and looked about eighteen.

Tips to make young executives look more experienced:

You can try adding gray temples, suggest growing beards, and wearing glasses but those strategies do not always work. Often, a youthful appearance is not the problem. It may be the "presenting problem" but it is not the underlying problem. Inexperience, wanting to be attractive to the opposite sex and lack of confidence often "leak" out in behavior, work habits, verbal content, speech patterns and body language.

- Work on the "mind-set" and make them aware of the young programming playing full blast in their head. Replace those beliefs with acknowledgment and appreciation of themselves and others. What do they *value* about themselves? Teach them to listen and acknowledge others instead of agonizing about how young they are, and see how their relationships improve.

- Change the casual clothes to an elegant casual look or even business dress. Casual clothes tend to make young people look less experienced. Opt for sharp lines and tailored silhouettes.

- Change the colors from pale and neutral to dark and rich. Upgrade fabrics from flimsy and inexpensive to a good quality. Good fabrics speak volumes for one's maturity.

- For women, banish barrettes, rubber bands, combs, banana clips, and hair ornaments. Recommend a great cut. If they cannot bear to have a single inch cut off, suggest great ways to put their hair up. For men, cut the hair short and get rid of fringes and bangs in the eyes, long wavy or curly locks, center parts, and long sideburns.

- Make sure the clothes fit. Fit is a very adult distinction in dress. Young people try to make clothes fit off the rack and often the garments look too tight, show too much skin, or are a little too sexy and low cut, or the skirts are too short. Even small alterations such as hemming the sleeves to the correct length, make all the difference.

- Suggest a light makeup. The barefaced schoolgirl look only goes so far and under fluorescent lights does nothing for their image. Studies have shown that women are 30% more likely to get the job if they wear makeup.

- Upgrade shirts from the collegiate Oxford button-down to shirts with straight collars in a smooth starched broadcloth or good cotton. Upgrade ties, pens, belts, shoes and wallets. Make sure every article is crisp and sharp. Youth comes with its own casual attitude, do not reinforce it.

- Work on verbal presentation skills. Pausing and ending the verbal message with eye contact, energy placement, use of personal space and judicious use of gestures will improve even the simplest of communications. Using a slower pace will also seem more self-confident. Rushing the message hoping to get through it fast is a sign of youth and nerves.

- Train them not to show their emotions on their face at every moment.

- Teach adult terminology such as "It's interesting that you say that." "You have a great point." Or, "By when can you get back to me?"

- Work with them on a great "elevator statement" with case studies and success stories, and have them practice it out loud. This should be a complete answer to the question, "What do you do?" that lasts about 30 seconds. They will need it for credibility, and more importantly, for their own confidence- building process.

- It is sometimes hard for young people to just be themselves. I heard a young man nervously trot out corporate jargon and he sounded like an orientation manual! Part of my training included practice in being natural. He needed to speak as he would to a friend even in presentations, using normal English and cutting out words like "like; feel; whatever…; out there…; ya know…; that is SOOO…"etc!

DISTINGUISHING LEVELS OF BUSINESS ATTIRE

With a decade of casual dress behind us, young people coming out of college have had no current model for formal business dress. Parents, teachers, and business people have all been wearing casual dress to work for as long as our college graduates can remember. Fashion magazines give them rather fanciful ideas of business dress but tend to err on the side of very current fashion, which is not always appropriate for either the interview or the workplace, even in a fashion industry. With so little guidance, high school and college leavers do not know what to wear. They often do not own a suit and come to the interview in casual clothes.

The best way to work with young people new to the working world is to introduce them to a tiered system of dress. Let them know that the clothes they are wearing are not wrong, just inappropriate for a serious attitude or promotion! The image industry seems to have come up with three to five types of dress.

LEVEL ONE

Formal Business Wear

The formal skirted suit for women in high levels of wool or blends, silk, polyester that looks like silk, refined cottons, silk knitwear and man made fibers for shells, shirts, and blouses. A pair of hose is mandatory, as are closed toed pumps; jewelry is small scale, refined, and silent! Hair is styled up or cut above the shoulders with a natural color, even if it is highlighted. For men, the single or double-breasted suit is still the most formal business dress. Silk ties in discreet patterns are most appropriate, as are dress shirt fabrics in high quality

cotton, short hairstyles, no facial hair and high-shine lace-up shoes. This is a look worn by politicians, heads of state, and their spouses, executives and heads of companies, high level interviewees, and professionals such courtroom lawyers and speakers or formal presenters.

LEVEL TWO

Top Level Casual

The next level always includes a jacket, or third piece, either tailored or un-constructed. This look would include a pantsuit, jacket or blazer and full-length slacks, closed toed pumps, sling-backs and trouser shoes for women, slip-ons, or loafers for men. The look might not need a tie for men if the shirt is designed without one and might also include a mock turtle or dress sweater or T-shirt under the jacket. Slacks for men are in wool or wool blends and mostly in darker shades. This look is appropriate for sales and marketing executives, managers and supervisors, TV anchors, speakers, trainers and interviews.

LEVEL THREE

Everyday Business Casual

The third level does not include a jacket
but always includes a collar for men.
The level is the most casual and is the
look worn currently by most employees.
It needs to be well coordinated with
good quality fabrics: well-cut and khaki
pants, black or grey jeans in great
condition; dress shirts or casual shirts
worn without a tie, sweaters and more
casual bomber jackets. For women, the
look includes twin sets, jersey pants, and
jackets, larger print or casual outer
layers, long skirts and tailored dresses.
This look is appropriate for levels below
management, people who do not meet
the public, customer service
representatives, IT employees.

Not appropriate in the business world:

- Exaggerated fashions
- Figure- clinging clothes
- Clothes revealing a lot of skin or
  cleavage
- Tattoos and body ornaments
- Loud or distracting jewelry
- Romantic dresses

- Transparent, evening, space age,
  or translucent fabrics
- Gym or sports clothes
- T-shirts
- Jeans unless part of the dress
  code and then they should be
  dress or designer jeans.

Chapter 4
BODY TALK

The Astonishing Communication of the Body

People have NO idea what their facial expressions or body posture are doing, (let alone projecting). When you coach clients on their body language, it is not enough to describe to them what to do.

Apart from clothing, we can help our clients in many other ways to enhance their personal and professional presence so they feel more effective and are perceived as such. One of the most powerful channels of communication is body language. Watch the way your clients walk, stand, and sit. Do they walk slowly or rapidly, forward or back, upright or bent forward, on the outside or inside of the foot, with straight knees or bent? What are the messages their physical walk and stance project? What is the body doing physically? Do they sink into their ribs when they stand, lean to one side or with a head cocked, or are their muscles rigid?

They need to practice simple physical changes on the spot or substitute other actions over and over. It will feel odd at first, but nothing is better than practicing. I once had a client who always looked like he was in pain and he often grimaced when he spoke, as if reacting to a muscle spasm. It was alarming to witness and you felt really sorry to see him suffering. It turned out that this was a facial muscle twitch he would do when searching for the right word, and he had absolutely no idea that his face was contorting. We worked to bring it to his conscious mind so that he could at least feel his facial muscles tightening. After several sessions, he substituted a chin raise movement and looked upwards the second he realized he was searching for a word. Fortunately, it did look much more normal.

NOTES:

YOUR SILENT FIRST IMPRESSION

A few years ago, I was approached by the president of a large international company with a knotty problem. His vice president of marketing had just been sent abroad to drum up business and it was not going well. Apparently the young man was interrupting loudly in sales presentations, backslapping comparative strangers, crunching ice from his glass, wringing the hand off the wrist every time he shook hands and never gave anyone direct eye contact. His business hosts were horrified and told the company to send someone with manners.

Even if you have mastered the idiosyncrasies of a foreign language there is another, equally important language to consider, especially in the business world. The nonverbal message or body language is the language of emotion and attitude. It can detract or enhance your spoken message and lend credibility to your words.

People actually decide whether they like you and want to do business with you based purely on the nonverbal messages you are sending. Your body language can make or break your professional success. It is certainly worthwhile to check out nonverbal customs and behavior so your clients do not unintentionally alienate a potential host, friend, associate, or boss.

Take facial expressions. In less than one fifth of a second the face can register an expression and then fade away. Fast and fleeting, these "micro expressions" can be the most important clues to the real but often almost unconscious emotion of a person. Because they are involuntary these expressions reveal the unspoken and underlying emotion, or that which is not being expressed openly in words. Human beings are bi-lingual in this astonishingly potent language, but our capacity to read them in others, particularly in strangers, gets rusty, just like our high school Spanish!

Paul Eckman and Wallace Friesen, the authorities on facial expressions and authors of *Unmasking the Face* (1975) have developed a scientific way to recognize and code every possible human expression with their Facial

Action Coding System or FACS. The FACS Atlas, available on CD-Rom describes all 43 "action units" able to be performed by the facial muscles, giving 10,000 documented facial expressions in all. Subtleties abound and unless we are students of the human face, babies, or stroke victims who have lost our speech, we can rarely distinguish one expression from another. For example, both anger and disgust have the eyebrows pulled down and the lips pressed hard together. In the case of disgust however, the nose is also wrinkled up. Surprise is similar to fear, except for one characteristic. In both expressions the eyebrows shoot up and the mouth opens. In surprise however, the lips are relaxed, like catching flies; with fear the mouth tightens and pulls back.

Paul Eckman's latest books are *Telling Lies* (2001); and *Emotions Revealed* (Spring 2004).

The ability to read facial expressions very quickly is a powerful tool for discerning emotion in interviews, litigation, sales, business dealings, negotiation, detective work, terrorism and in communication with our friends, families, and associates. Full facial expressions rarely last more than .5 to 2.5 seconds. That is the duration of a blink! Some are so rapid and sometimes affect such a small portion of the face that they are displayed even before the mind has had a chance to register them. These fleeting expressions are probably the most honest signals. If you catch them, even subliminally, you might get a "funny feeling" about the conversation, because you register that at least one of the expressions does not match the verbal message. Facial flashes such as being startled, in despair, angry or afraid for example, in an otherwise neutral dialogue, are known as "leakage." Practiced face-watchers like detectives or spy catchers can spot microsecond flashes of emotion on the face. Combined with small shifts in eye contact and body posture or slight changes of verbal communication such as swallows, speech pauses and repetitions the total emotional package can be uncovered. Once they get a hunch from these minute clues that the victim is hiding something, they can press to the root of the issue.

Humans have also developed an uncanny knack for covering up their true expressions. With the technique of a practiced poker player we have learned to pull our own skin around with our attached facial muscles and create expressions that cover up the underlying emotion. Take the smile for example. It is probably our oldest expression and is used to disarm, reassure, and to demonstrate that we come in friendship, not aggression. Our smile muscles are 90% "fast-twitch" fibers, compared to the frown muscle that is only 50% fast-twitch. It is almost twice as much work to frown than to smile, and our faces know it! The smile can appear on the face even when we are frightened, the combination of which appears as a grimace like the "fear-grin" of monkeys.

The variations of body posture and gestures also provide a richness of language and a key to the emotions. In the rash of corporate frauds and cover-ups at the beginning of the millennium, photos in the media of the guilty executives spoke volumes. At first these people had upright, militant postures, chins jutting out and fixed tight smiles.

Once foiled and found guilty however, their bodies seem to crumple up, their chests cave in, the smiles fade, and their fingers are tightly closed, often covering their faces. A submissive posture is always closed in, head down with no eye contact. Joseph Berardino, during the review process of Arthur Andersen sat collapsed in his chair as though all the air had gone out of him. Jeffrey Skilling of Enron defended himself at first with his hands outstretched and fingers wide. Later as things looked less optimistic, he testified with his hand covering his mouth and little eye contact. You would have gained the same impression with the sound on the TV completely muted.

In contrast, politicians in the recent caucuses have had their arms punching high into the air, their fingers clenched into fists for power, or arms outstretched and palms open for honesty. As much as Martha Stewart wanted us to think she was in control, she walked through the paparazzi with a half-smile, eyes darting, not quite knowing where to look, all of which has made her look rather dazed and scared but trying to brave it out.

There are two very important aspects to nonverbal communication. First, it is uncanny how a change of nonverbal language on our part: gestures, stance, posture and facial expressions, can influence and affect our own self-image. Apparently we can influence our own thinking, feelings, and even self-confidence. Second, it is even more astounding how our nonverbal language affects and influences the attitude of others towards us. Studies have established a connection between our body language and the extent to which people are influenced by the content of our verbal communication.

Doctors come under harsh criticism for having a good or bad bedside manner, and indeed most medical schools have traditionally devoted little if any time to this aspect of patient communication. In fact, when we speak to people about our doctor or any professional for that matter, we often only describe our experience of the appointment, the trust level with the medical professional and the feeling we get from the doctor. Unless people want to pile up evidence against the doctor they don't often recount with enormous detail their training, credentials and the number of errors they have made.

When my father was very sick and couldn't get to the office, his general practitioner made a house visit. I was impressed that the medical man still made house calls and built high hopes that he could help my dad. Unfortunately, when he arrived, he turned out to have the personality of a turnip. He sat in a chair quite far away from us, said very little, never smiled, hardly asked questions, wrote out a couple of prescriptions and left after ten minutes. He subsequently did all the right things and certainly had all the right credentials, but my father lost all faith in him, and his condition deteriorated. Luckily Dad was referred to another specialist, a consultant who had lots of energy and seemed concerned. The physician, leaned forward, and even touched my father's arm from time to time. He had sparkling eyes and excellent eye contact. He laughed and joked, and helped my dad into and out of his chair. The difference in *my father* was quite amazing. In response, Dad also leaned forward, his eyes brightened and he held strong eye contact and smiled with the consultant. His energy level increased and he joked a little. That day, he even went out to lunch for the first time in many months and his condition improved slowly from that visit on.

A study done by medical researcher Wendy Levinson studied the difference between patient-doctor conversations. She included two groups of doctors in her sample: those doctors who had never been sued and those who had been sued at least twice. The credentials, training, and number of medical mistakes made by the doctors were the same. Yet the team found obvious differences between the two groups. The differences lay with their nonverbal practices and body language. In other words, the way they treated the patient personally. Non-sued doctors spent more than three minutes longer with each patient (18.3 minutes versus 15 minutes.); they laughed and were funny, listened actively, asked questions and made orienting comments such as: "First, I'll examine you, then we will talk it over." And "Tell me more

about that." (Wendy Levinson et al, "*Physician-Patient Communication: The Relationship with Malpractice Claims Among Primary Care Physicians and Surgeons.*" Journal of the American Medical Association 277.No.7 (1997), 553-559.)

Psychologist Nalini Ambady took this same study one step further. She took 40-second clips of the doctor talking to the patient and "content-filtered" the clips, removing content but leaving the sounds such as pronunciation, intonation, pitch, and rhythm. A team of judges evaluated the garbled segments of speech on qualities such as warmth, hostility, dominance, and anxiousness. Although the analysis was purely on tone of voice the results were extremely interesting. They found that they could predict which doctors were in the sued group and which weren't. If the doctor sounded "dominant," they were likely to be in the sued group; if he sounded "concerned," he was likely to be in the non-sued group. In this case the tone of voice alone was the clue to the first impression, an impression that really had profound consequences and legal ramifications. Medical schools would be well served to include nonverbal communication as part of their curriculum. Alternatively, we could approach this as a rich target market for our services!

Nalini Ambady et al., "*Surgeons' Tone of Voice: A Clue to Malpractice History*," Surgery 132, No 1 (2002): 5-9

We as image consultants can start practicing face and body watching. We can study people in airports, in the grocery line, on television and in the newspapers. It is a useful tool and an exceptional service for our clients. Put your clients on video and let them watch their own face and body. Use a close-up camera and stop the video when you get to a telling moment. We can all see how fleeting yet powerful that flash of micro-expression or down- turned mouth can be to counter a seemingly upbeat verbal message. Similarly, it is also amazing how our body language can enhance and emphasize the spoken word. Teach people these secrets and you will have new skills and services to offer them.

NONVERBAL WAYS TO ACCESS YOUR POWER

Posture

The most visible way to communicate confidence is in your ability to control valuable space. The position of your neck, The amount of lift in your ribs The straightness of your knees are all responsible for the quality of the posture. A good posture promotes self-confidence and shows that you are comfortable in your own space or "bubble."

Smile

We can smile even when we are terrified in order to fool our enemies! The smile is the universal expression common to all greetings and even monkeys have a "fear-grin." A raise of the eyebrows plus smile denotes an open attitude and is also recognized globally.

Handshake

There are many variations on the handshake, a form of which originated in Roman times, when men locked hand to upper arm and were actually feeling for daggers. A handshake has since become a token gesture meaning that we come to the relationship without weapons, in friendship and are willing for someone to touch us.

Touch

Touch itself is an intimate interaction for humans and an interesting human phenomenon. Gentle pressure denotes affection but the same gesture with a stronger pressure can be hostile. When the level of pressure does not match the message, we are confused, such as the cheek- pinch that we all dreaded as kids or the playful slap or bone-crusher handshake.

Keep Hands Dry

People react to the moisture content in your skin and the strength of your grip. Keep your hands dry and warm if you want to be cool and have a firm but not overly strong handshake.

Head-Cock

The female head cock (head on one side) is related to the childlike posture of laying the head on the chest of the mother and is always considered coy, flirtatious, young, or innocent. Keep your head straight if you want to appear poised, in control and professional.

Kissing

Kissing originates from the practice of the mother who chewed the food before she gave it to her baby. Obviously, the farther way from the mouth, the less intimate the intent of the kiss. Years ago, hand kissing became a substitute for an ardent admirer to show his admiration and it is still practiced in some countries. Don't be surprised if a Frenchman or Italian presses your knuckles to his mouth accompanied with a bow!

Nervousness

When we feel nervous or threatened we will automatically protect ourselves by closing in and drawing our arms high around our body. This "relic" is a leftover gesture from childhood when we consoled ourselves by self-hugging and rocking to protect ourselves from harm. To look composed when speaking in public, stand straight, rest your arms on your hipbones and loosely cross your fingers just below the waist.

Crossing the Arms

The arms-crossed, protection posture seems odd if we are having a comfortable conversation with a friend. Strange as it may seem, if you uncross your arms, you will notice how your own attitude changes slightly during the conversation. That is a very simple example of how body language can

actually shape attitude and affect the relationship, as much as the other way around.

Covering the Mouth

We tend to cover our mouths when we are uncertain of ourselves or threatened. This comes from childhood when we stuck our thumb or fingers in our mouths for comfort. Keep your hands away from the face when speaking and keep gestures chest level or below and appropriate to the message.

Covering up in General

If we are trying to cover up our fear the "leakage" can be felt and even seen in tense shoulders and limbs. Our smile becomes glued onto our face and we can't relax. An old maxim says trust the part of the body farthest from the face! Exercise and yoga will help relax the muscles.

Yawning

If you think of the yawn, you can see how we influence each other with body language alone. When you yawn, I yawn too! The yawn does in fact have a biological function. It causes a slight rise in heartbeat and increased circulation to improve the blood supply to the brain. If you yawn the body is craving more oxygen. Stand up and move!

Copycat Gestures

Human beings often unconsciously copy the postures and gestures of others, especially if they feel a rapport with another. We are saying, "I am like you and I am your equal in status." Slow moving film or video clips show clearly the extent to which we demonstrate synchronicity with our friends or with those with whom we sense a rapport. William Condon in the 1960's studied cultural micro rhythms from carefully studying segments of film showing people in families speaking to each other. He found that patterns of gestures emerged in what he called "interact ional synchrony." The patterns were repeated by the speaker many times, not only in response to his own words and sentences but also in response to other's talking. They were, over the course of a conversation, in perfect harmony with themselves and each other; rather as if they were all participating in a well rehearsed dance. Condon found that everyone in his filmed conversation made these movements within one to three 1/45th of a second frame of the film. The same eye-flicks, head-dips, shoulder moves, hands, and body movements were made all within split seconds of each other. Subsequently it has been found that all this information is carried to the cortex to create feelings of warmth, and rapport. Other studies and films of mental patients and serial killers on the other hand have shown no such synchronicity of gestures and posture with others around them.

Notice your body language and that of your companions. How similar is it? Certain schools of thought tell us to copy our partner's posture to create rapport. However, the synchronicity in these studies suggests that the subtle dance or harmony has to be induced naturally. Anything conscious would seem too artificial. It may be more appropriate to concentrate on creating rapport with the spoken word and let the nonverbal dance follow naturally.

We all have a well-defined "bubble" around us into which we will invite others. We even have the term "arms akimbo" when we define our space, increase our space, and remind people to keep out. It is a global posture, usually denoting defiance or aggression and would not be useful in a business setting. Pointing and jabbing a finger in someone's face are also invasions of the bubble. Pointing of any sort is an unacceptable gesture in the Chinese culture. Use the back of your hand outstretched, to indicate that your attention is on someone or something.

In a crowded elevator your "bubble" is seriously violated. To protect ourselves against strangers we shrink into the smallest size, give no eye contact, and fall silent. The size of the bubble grows depending on the situation. The intimate zone is 0 feet to 1.5 feet when touch may occur, but **only** if we allow it. The personal zone is 1.5 feet to 4 feet, the distance between two people chatting or shaking hands. The social zone is four to 10 feet and the public zone 10 feet and beyond.

Clients often ask: "How can I tell if someone is lying?" Well the indicators are subtle, not very reliable, and very inconclusive. However, there are some lying clues:

- Hand goes to the mouth
- Fleeting loss of eye contact
- Hand movements are suppressed
- Body shifts
- Hand shrug used as a disclaimer
- Imperceptible delays of expression accompanying the words
- Stammering or use of fillers.

None of these is conclusive evidence of lying but all may denote an inner conflict or a discomfort with the words spoken.

Walk the Walk

Walks are difficult to change. We learned to walk as a toddler and our walk has evolved over time and hardened into a carriage and gate that is shaped by our self-image.

A good walk should push off the back foot onto a straight front leg. If you step onto a wobbly, bent front knee with your weight pitched forward, head down, you look as though you are walking up hill or in a perpetual hurry. In a self-confident walk, the back foot peels off the floor and the knee bends with a smooth movement as the foot pulls through to the front. The front heel should then be placed on the floor on a line with the heel of the back foot, toes slightly turned out. The front thigh and knee should then be straight and the thigh and gluteus maximus (bottom) muscles involved. The weight of the top body should feel as though it's slightly behind the hips as you transfer weight. You should feel the three parts of the foot flat on the floor as you walk: big toe, little toe, and heel. The chin is level and the head relaxed. Your head should be straight over your shoulders, not pushed forward, or tipped over; your ears, shoulders, hips, and ankles should be in alignment. The stride needs to be short so that the body feels secure and upright. If you teach your clients to walk and stand correctly, they will be amazed at the difference in self-confidence they not only project, but also experience. The physical positioning alters the way they think about themselves and the world. Try it for yourself.

Chapter 5

IMAGE FOR THE INTERVIEW

One of the ways our work can be applied most effectively is to coach clients who are in the process of interviewing or on an upwardly mobile career path. When faced with stiff competition, the majority of interviewees realize that their appearance, interview responses, and nonverbal communication play a critical role in differentiating them from the other candidates.

An interesting study was done in 1986 by Brian Mullen et al. "Newscasters' facial expressions and voting behavior of viewers: Can a smile elect a president?" Journal of Personality and Social Psychology (1986) vol. 51, pp 291-295. Just before the 1984 Reagan-Mondale elections Mullen took TV clips of Peter Jennings (ABC), Dan Rather (CBS) and Tom Brokaw, (NBC). The topic of every clip was about the political candidates. In all there were 37 clips, each two and a half minutes in length. He showed them with no sound to the study subjects who were asked to rate the facial expressions on a negative-neutral-positive emotional scale. Dan Rather and Brokaw scored neutral for both candidates. Jennings on the other hand scored neutral for Mondale and positive for Reagan. The study concluded that Jennings had a "significant and noticeable bias in facial expression" towards Reagan. The second part of the study is telling. After the election, Mullen, and colleagues called people around the country and asked what station they watched the news and who they voted for. In every case, those who watched ABC with Peter Jennings voted in greater numbers for Reagan. In another study, vigorous head nodding, head shaking or neutral stance influenced and affected a later outcome, not even connected to the first experiment. The simple action of head shaking elicited negative feelings towards a proposition; the head neutrals were neutral towards it and the head nodders were in favor.

Gary Wells and Richard Petty: "The Effect of Overt Head Movements on Persuasion." Basic and Applied Social Psychology (1980) vol. 1 no. 3 pp 219-230.

These two studies illustrate on an extremely subtle level the bias that body language can promote. Though we do not realize we are being influenced by our own body language or by that of others, we are. Think of the implications in an interview. Positive body language on the part of the candidate, even more than the spoken word might influence the decision of the interviewer, far more than they are aware of. Our job as image consultants is to train our clients to such an extent that they deliver their content effectively, authentically and meaningfully. The words, tone, style, and nonverbal delivery must be congruent, as one, seamless and well honed.

The National Association of Colleges and Employers specializes in information about the college market and conducts an annual study as part of its *Job Outlook 2002*. This association.

On the surveys of 457 employers that recruit new college graduates, an overwhelming:

- 92% revealed that "a candidate's overall appearance" influences their opinion about the candidate."

- 82% reported being negatively influenced when a candidate wears "nontraditional" attire to the job interview.

- 73% are turned off by "unusual" hair color. Purple was specifically mentioned.

- 72% can't tolerate body piercing. Nose rings and lip studs are too decorative for a business office, say the folks who do their hiring.

- 60% object to "obvious" tattoos.

- 64% don't' like "unusual" hairstyles.

How you look is a factor in whether or not you get the job you want, and whether you are hired as a consultant. How can we affect our clients' appearance to streamline their way to successful business relationships? This information was taken from an article published in April 22, 2002 in the Hartford Courant.

DRESS

When it comes to the interview, most employers expect the interviewee to look the best he can muster! Although the company personnel may be dressed more casually than you expect, your potential business colleagues or interviewer will expect you to be in business dress. Make sure that your client represents himself or herself in the best light and they appear to have taken this meeting seriously. Visual impact, or the first impression is very important in an interview. Clothes send messages and indeed, people make profound value judgments about each other based purely on superficial evidence such as dress and appearance. If they are oddly dressed, sloppy, untidy, or extremely fashionable, it might count against them in the interview. An interviewer may have read their resume or Curriculum Vitae and will have formed some expectations from it. Do they now live up to the story and reputation that precedes them?

The first rule of thumb would be to err on the side of conservative tailored styling. For example women should wear classic dresses, jackets, suits, and pantsuits. Men should wear suits, jackets, and slacks that have a classic, western cut. Fabric, accessories, garment construction, and good fit all denote the level of quality and communicate messages. People should invest in high quality fabrics for the interview. Hose for women and ties for men are recommended. Men's hair is short for a business image and facial hair is far less common in business than in the engineering and artistic industries or the medical or architectural professions.

Do not suggest clothes that are too ethnic or unusual because the people interviewing might not view them in the same way. Dripping with too much precious jewelry might send a message of ostentation. Body rings or tattoos and heavy leather send the message of gang warfare! Clothes that are soiled, crumpled, torn, or worn out also project negative messages to the interviewer, demonstrating nonverbally that they do not care about the situation at hand and do not respect the process.

INTERVIEW FAUX PAS:

Interviewee displays	Interviewer thinks
Dragon-Lady fingernails, fancy patterned or brightly colored hose, wild prints or jangling jewelry.	*"Leave the Halloween costumes in the basement."*
Strong cologne or aftershave.	*"You smell like my ex...and the interview goes downhill.*
Hair covering the eyes, wild hairstyles, or psychedelic shades.	*"Hair today, gone tomorrow."*
Short sleeved shirts, with or without the tie.	*"I'm Bruce, your captain today...."*
Bright socks, heavy evening makeup, after hours fabrics and clothes.	*The hours here are actually 8:30 am to 5:00 pm.*
Too Much Skin	*Too Much Information.*
Conversation ties. Try an elegant geometric, foulard, paisley, or Repp tie.	*So what if you were a Dead Head back in the 70's!*
Flip-flops, sandals, and bare legs.	*And the way to the beach is...?*
Five o'clock shadow. ...	*Did you forget to shave or have you just risen for the day?"*
Carrying an oversized tote, purse, bags, backpack, and sunglasses on the head or on the face, I-pods, headphones or fanny packs....	*Bag ladies of the world, unite! You have nothing to lose but this interview.*
Visible tattoos, nose, or other facial piercing.	*Did they tie you to your desk in your last company?*
Dated dress.	*And so are your ideas.*
Loud "Drug Lord" jewelry on men.	*"I see business is picking up."*

The interviewers want to be assured that your clients will be a valuable asset to the company and align with the values of the company. Your clients could be asked questions about sports, family and preferences as well as the business at hand. Make sure they have done their homework and know the answers to these questions. They should never be asked about politics, sex or religion, their age or why they left the last job.

Your clients should answer the interviewer with direct eye contact; sitting up comfortably with a straight back against the back of the chair, hands in lap that will give the impression of energy, vitality and intention. A slumped or rigid posture, no direct eye contact, distracting hand and arm movements, covering the face or mouth with the hands and excessive fidgeting will all be strikes against them.

Make sure your client has organized all essential papers in a single folder, where they are accessible and easy to find. They should take out all unnecessary documents, notes and forms. Under pressure and nerves, we tend to make

mistakes and fail to notice and forget critical things. It is important that your client is organized enough to produce information quickly and with ease.

Recommend that they research the company and find out the expected dress code for interviews. If the organization is in solid lower-end casual and would think of them as a freak in a suit, suggest a jacket and dress pants and they may have to remove the jacket.

Finally, school your clients in courtesy, flexibility, and patience. The process might take longer than expected, so they should not plan important meetings or events on the same day and leave plenty of time to find the location.

Verbal Secrets to Successful Interviews

1. Illustrate everything you say with quantifiable evidence. Research facts, figures, and percentages from previous paid or non-paid positions. To say, "I increased sales," is not enough. By what percentage did you increase sales? Are you referring to revenues or

profits? How did this compare to your competition: was it a good year all round or did you specifically perform a sterling job? What situations did you have to overcome: How did you do that?

2. Don't just say that you are good at communication or team building or management, give solid examples to demonstrate. For example on management communication skills: "I instigated a department-wide policy on complaints. When employees had a grievance, they wrote it out with a possible solution and put it into a box. We incorporated their complaints into the next staff meeting."

3. Prepare five to ten case studies from your previous employment or life experience. These are now examples at your fingertips to illustrate every point you make about your experience, skills, talents, and capacities. Rest assured you would not sound arrogant if you have the proof to back up every statement.

TOP TEN INTERVIEW MISTAKES

1. *Rambling, incoherent, off the subject, and not answering the question asked.*

2. *Not listening and having to have the question repeated.*

3. *"Tape recorder" and pre-set answers. Yes, prepare but make it sound spontaneous!*

4. *Betraying your own agenda rather than illustrating how your skills can contribute to the organization: E.g., "I am just applying to get the vacation benefits."*

5. *Not doing any research about the job or the company.*

6. *Gossiping and complaining about previous co-workers.*

7. *Demonstrating little interest for the position.*

8. *Tooting your own horn without any substantiating evidence.*

9. *Bad posture; dark glasses throughout the interview; intoxicated; wearing jeans and dirty T-shirt, dirty fingernails.*

10. *Exaggerating achievements or misrepresenting the facts on the resume.*

BODY LANGUAGE CRITICAL IN INTERNATIONAL BUSINESS

A steady eye contact is your most powerful listening tool. Studies have shown that you will be considered more sympathetic, intelligent and compassionate if you have a steady gaze. Eye contact in the western world is extremely important and the lack of it denotes low self-confidence, fear and even a shifty attitude. People feel they can trust you if you use frequent eye contact and at least 2 -3 seconds long. Do not cover up your eyes with dark or tinted glasses since people are unconsciously looking for pupil dilation to register your interest in them and what they are saying.

Do shake hands in an appropriate manner

Stay at 2-3 feet away from your companion or about a relaxed arm's length. Make contact with the other person's hand so that your web or the skin between thumb and first finger is touching his. Do not clutch just the ends of his fingers. Hold his hand with a firm grip and pump the arm once or twice, no more. The web of your hands should be facing directly upwards. Gentlemen, do not turn her hand over or put your second hand on top of hers.

If you find you are nervous, wash your hands just before the meeting, to make sure they are not sweating or clammy!

Do stand up and sit up straight but not stiff or rigid

A slumping posture is interpreted as an uncaring attitude, weakness of character or boredom. A rigid posture denotes nervousness or confrontation. It is difficult to build rapport when you interpret the body language as anything but positive and enthusiastic. Good posture says that you are confident. Remember that your body movements tend to be jerky and uncoordinated when you are nervous. To compensate for this unwanted muscular reaction, breathe much deeper than usual to allow more oxygen to enter the blood stream. Professional speakers and actors need to activate synapses from both brain hemispheres so that they quickly attain optimum performance levels and relax the muscles at the same time. Try this exercise. While standing, bring one knee up and across the body until you can touch the opposite elbow. Repeat on the opposite side. Do this exercise at a fast pace at least 20 times. Your heart rate will increase and your muscles will relax.

Do smile warmly

A warm smile is one that comes from the eyes and not just the mouth. Focus your attention on the other person's eyes and nowhere else during the greeting. Your smile should last as long as your eye contact and handshake, even if you have to shake hands with many people, otherwise it does not seem sincere.

Do not be late

Time is a precious commodity and you are expected to be punctual. In a business scenario, if you are delayed more than 10 minutes, be sure to call and communicate with the person you are meeting. If you are not sure where you are going, try a "dry run" the day before to time the length of the trip in traffic and orient yourself.

Socially, you have a longer grace period, but again, call if you are going to be over 20 to 30 minutes late for a dinner party.

Do listen actively and intently to your companion

It is considered ill mannered to listen without eye contact. If your eyes are darting all around you your companion will get the impression that you are more interested in your surroundings than in him and he will think you are rude. In a listening posture, you would be still, have steady eye contact, (try focusing on one eye not both), tilt your head, nod at intervals and murmur "uh-huh" to show that you are paying attention. Your hands should be resting in your lap with the fingers open not clenched shut. Do not cross your arms or turn away when you are in a conversation with one person. Closed body language in close proximity is considered a barrier to the relationship and has a negative impact on the person talking.

RESUME FAUX PAS

The following is a collection of extracts taken from real resumes…really!

(*Source unknown*)

- "References: None. I left a path of destruction behind me."
- It's best for employers that I don't work with people.
- "I procrastinate, especially when the task is unpleasant."
- Reason for leaving last job: maturity leave."
- "Marital status: Often, Children: various."
- I have lurnt Word perfect 6.0 computor and spreasheet prgroms."
- Note: Please don't misconstrue my 14 jobs as "job-hopping." I have never quit a job."

Here are some real quotes from employers' performance evaluations:

- "Since my last report, this employee has reached rock bottom and has started to dig."
- "This employee is depriving a village somewhere of an idiot."
- "I would not allow this employee to breed."
- "He sets low personal standards and then consistently fails to achieve them."
- "This employee should go far, and the sooner he starts, the better."
- "When she opens her mouth, it seems that this is only to change whichever foot was previously in there."

Chapter 6

ADDING COACHING TO YOUR SERVICES

Have you noticed that your advice in image often spills over to other life habits? If you continue to find that your clients have issues that cannot be handled in an individual image consultation, and you are looking for ways to expand your business, consider becoming a project-based coach to your client.

Project based coaching is oriented towards goals and results, and will provide a structure for your clients to fulfill their goals more effectively and quicker than they would on their own. Male executives especially prefer females when it comes to choosing a coach (*Male Execs like Female Coaches*, by Del Jones, USA Today, November 21st 2001). If your client isn't familiar with the coaching process, it will be useful to explain how it works.

An excellent structure is a pre-coaching form. This will ask questions such as what they would like to get out of the coaching. You might also set out the ground rules to clarify the relationship. These will include the payment schedule and your fees; you expect them to keep all calls or appointments; your policy on rescheduling; they must complete assignments and do all homework. Ask permission to uncover any underlying roadblocks that have prevented them from being successful in the past. Let them know you are not going to be easy going and let anything slide!

Sample Questions for Pre-Coaching Form

Full Name, Nickname, Address, all phone numbers; e-mail address; best times to contact;

Have you had any previous coaching experience?

For what?

What were the outcomes?

Rating your performance, could the experience have been improved?

What do you want to gain from this coaching arrangement?

What are the projects involved?

What are the desired results?

Do you know if you work best in longer or shorter sessions?

What is your track record on completing tasks/homework?

Fee structure:

Payment Dates:

Suggested Ground Rules:

X sessions per month. Unlimited/restricted e-mail and personal contact. *(You choose)*

Payment is due before the sessions.

Cancellations are to be communicated 12 hours in advance or payment will be incurred.

No-shows will be billed.

The client calls the coach at the appointed time. If the phone is busy, wait five minutes and call back.

Complete homework is expected by the following session.

We expect you to do all assignments or else communicate or negotiate.

Do not gossip about the sessions

I agree to abide by these ground rules.

……………………………….Signed………………..Date

How do you structure a project-based coaching relationship?

Decide on the issue to be addressed such as weight loss, a workout schedule or coaching for an interview	Set it up as a project, with a time limit and goals. Set goals on both a weekly and monthly basis.
Coaching often includes homework between calls, unlike a mentor or counselor who might give sporadic advice. Start each coaching session by aligning with the client what is to be accomplished by the end of the session.	Your goal as a coach is to make sure that measurable results are produced in the time frame set. Give homework in between sessions and always debrief it.
Be committed to the client's success. Keep the client focused on what is important to her. People actually forget what they are committed to, what their vision was and why they are doing this or that project in the first place!	Allow for exploration and discovery of new ideas but keep your attention on the vision.
Listen on many levels.	A. Listen to the content of the words. B. Listen to the sub-text or the underlying message behind the words: tone, vocabulary, pauses, and inflection might all express hidden emotions, unpleasant past experiences and fear or anger. These are all limitations or roadblocks to the current success. If your client is ever going to grow beyond those limitations, you must have the courage to address them and break them open. Are they aware of the underlying issue? Are they committed to action and willing to set out an action plan within a time frame. Your job is to whittle all that out of them and set homework to address and push through those limitations.

How do you structure a project-based coaching relationship?

	C. Listen to the radio in your own head. What judgments and opinions are you bringing to this conversation? Are you imposing your own opinions, points of view and emotions on the conversation?
Ask questions rather than being too ready to supply answers, solutions or advice. Sometimes you might have to volunteer your opinion if it's appropriate, but on the whole, let your client do the work.	Keep bringing the analogy of the personal trainer to the conversation. I have never noticed that my personal trainer picks up the weights and pumps the iron for me! Furthermore, the answer always lies with the owner of the issue
The conversation is a delightful dance between the two of you. Keep it light and humorous. Use silence to your advantage.	You should be enlivened after a session, not tired
At the end of every session, put in a structure to make your client accountable. What will they accomplish by the next session? "What, by when?" is your best friend.	Make requests and get straight answers, such as "Yes" and "No." Cut out excuses, rationales and soap operas
Always set a date and time for the calls and let them call you.	All coaching should be paid for in advance. It helps people listen more attentively. You can charge by the session, the week or the month. Fees range from $50-$750 per hour!
A session might run 1/2 to 1-1/2 hours. Shorter sessions, more often can be more effective than a few long sessions spaced out, especially if the client loses focus easily or the goals are imminent	
When you have accomplished the goals of that project, celebrate victories and failures.	Debrief the project with your client and get closure: what worked, what did not work?

TROUBLESHOOTING

If the client is not keeping her appointments, address that issue immediately. Ask her if the sessions are useful, if you have offended her in any way, or whether the structure you have set up to talk regularly is working for her. What would she like to communicate to you? Have you created a "safe space" for her to confide, or are you a judgmental undercover agent if she isn't perfect? I have heard people complain that their coaches are "brutal!" You can be rigorous with your client and not let her off the hook, but you always need to be compassionate and light.

If your client isn't doing her assignments, she is probably stuck about something. Either she doesn't know how to do them or there is something blocking her pathway. She might have forgotten what she took on the coaching for, especially if life is now overwhelming. In that case take her back to the original form she wrote out. (Make sure you have a pre-coaching form.) What was her original purpose and intention for the coaching? Your coaching now needs to include some time management and prioritization skills.

Perhaps the inspiration and motivation has evaporated! Very likely, if she isn't doing the work! Get her back on track with a tighter schedule and ask her to report back more often, daily if that is appropriate.

You may have stumbled upon a critical issue that shows up everywhere in her life. For example, she has tried to lose weight before and can't do it. Unearthing the real issue might be the key here, which might be something she is ashamed to divulge. The excuses and justifications always cloak the issue. I was coaching a young lady on weight loss and she had a number of excuses and rationales as to why she couldn't lose weight: Problems with the boyfriend; had to have chocolate when she was tired; couldn't lose weight because of all the stress; would go to parties and drink one glass of wine and eat herself silly! We ploughed the depths and she finally got to the fact that she never kept her promises to herself. She would be fine if she was accountable to a boss, coworker, a family member or a friend, but never when there was no one else involved. The underlying tape was: "I don't count!" and "I'll be a good girl if you are watching me." She wrote a daily record of examples where she didn't keep her word to herself and put in a plan to overcome every one. She then appointed someone to whom she could report progress. Very soon, with such a rigorous structure she got used to keeping her word. When she said she would buy certain foods, she did. When she said she would write out a meal plan for the week, she handed it in.

When she had a party coming up she took her own low calorie sparkling apple cider to the event! She boxed herself in, but the eating plan was not so strict that it didn't include treats. She was also so busy sticking to the plan that she literally didn't have time for excuses.

Chapter 7
DRESS CODES

You will find this legal information helpful when you are selling your consulting services to a company. Even employers and human resource professionals are not always aware of their legal position when it comes to dress codes. Here are some guidelines covering the minimum legal requirements and rights. When in doubt, consult a labor lawyer or the company legal department.

Employers have the right to develop a company dress code and make employment decisions based on how individuals dress and groom. "Individuals," in legal documents refer to all employees, exempt, non-exempt, full-time, part-time, temporary, new or regular. A dress and grooming code may be based on any health, safety or other legitimate business reason such as business needs and job functions.

Guidelines for permissible dress:

- May require employees to dress consistent with the company's image.
- May prohibit inappropriate clothing and appearances.
- Must not interfere with employees' labor rights.

COMPANY IMAGE

An example would be Mr. Smith, an employer who requires his sales people to wear business suits and his warehouse employees to wear blue shirts and steel-toed shoes. His secretary greets visitors and often accompanies him to conferences. He may ask her to wear clothing appropriate to the company image. He could also ask her to wear a company T-shirt or blazer with a logo that promotes the company identity when she is at work or representing the company out of the office.

Inappropriate Clothing and Appearance

Employers may restrict or prohibit inappropriate fashions, hairstyles, jewelry, tattoos and other dress and grooming items. Ms. Jenkins, the Human Resource Manager interviews a young man who is a promising candidate. However his arms are covered with tattoos and she is uncomfortable and distracted by the adornment and thinks that customers will be too. She may not hire him on those grounds or she may hire him on the condition that he covers his arms. If he fails to comply with that written rule, she may discipline him or even fire him as a violator.

As a guideline for all employees, Ms. Jenkins may develop and adopt a dress code. As long as employees' appearances are within their control, employers may prohibit any fashion or display such as nose rings, unusual hair color or multiple earrings that the company deems inappropriate and inconsistent with its image. For example, the dress code may require employees to cover themselves and not expose inappropriate parts of their body.

However, to avoid an invasion of privacy, the code may not state exactly how this should be done. Again, if employees have body odor or wear unclean clothes the employer is within his rights to ask those individuals to improve their cleaning habits.

The only exemption from the dress and appearance code may be if the employee has a documented medical condition, such as foot surgery. In this case, written documentation that goes into the employee's file is recommended.

Employee Labor Rights

Employers may also impose reasonable limits necessary for production or safety reasons. For example, dangling earrings and long hair may pose a safety threat to a factory worker whose job requires her to be close to moving parts machinery. Employers in the food industry generally require employees working with food to tie their hair back and even to wear a hairnet. If a hospital uniform code disallows non-regulation pins and other jewelry then the employer may discipline employees who disregard the rules.

However, employers may not prohibit their employees from wearing union buttons or other signs related to their labor rights.

Writing a dress code

If you are asked to write a dress and appearance code, say yes! Using these basic guidelines you can create a viable, legal dress code.

For example, one airline we consulted with had gone to great trouble to train all the employees in the new rules, such as acceptable skirt lengths, heel height, hairstyle, shoes and accessories. After a year employees had slipped back into their old habits. The company thought the campaign had failed. We said no, not necessarily. All they needed was to adopt structures *consistently* and *continuously* to implement the rules. Human beings forget and take the most convenient, comfortable way out!

We worked with their supervisors and managers to help them get everyone back on track and establish consequences without coming across like the fashion police! The first question asked was: "Are you aware of the dress code and compliance rules?" If no, they would be given a copy and a timeframe in which they could comply. If yes, they were asked what **they** could do about their infringement. The responsibility was all theirs. This went a long way towards the successful buy-in of the program by the vast majority of employees. Eventually, there were occasional examples of people breaking the rules, but these became the exception not the norm and nonverbal peer pressure became a great deterrent.

Guidelines for writing Dress Codes

If candidates are given a copy of the dress code somewhere during the hiring or orientation process and an opportunity to sign off on the rules, compliance will go much more smoothly.

In addition to the code, rules or guidelines, a code will be much more effective if the company also develops consequences for non-compliance. These can be as simple as a warning for the first offence, written up for the second and told to go home and change on the third. If stricter measures are needed you can work with the H.R. or legal department or consult a labor lawyer in your area.

You can suggest ways to implement the code. A memo from HR or even the CEO is rarely sufficient. A more effective approach is to devise a whole fun campaign over a period of time. This campaign should start with a broadcast of the reasons and benefits behind the initiative, introduced by the message of consistency with the corporate image and *what exactly the corporate image is*! Seminars and backup reminders in the newsletter or other company communication may be needed as reinforcement. Photographs on the bulletin board illustrating the correct outfit and garment details are valuable visuals to promote the message. The rollout might start with a one-month probationary period when every violator is given a warning and a copy of the new dress code. After that, the disciplinary action takes over.

Remember by law, the employer has the right to decide what is and what is not consistent with the company image and can ask the employees to change if it is within their control to do so.

Use the categories of business dress as the basis of your guidelines.
For example acceptable business dress could be in three major categories:

- Level 1, Formal business dress, such as the suit for men and the skirted suit for women.
- Level 2, Tailored jacket and pants for men or pantsuit and jacket and tailored pants for women.
- Level 3. Basic Business Casual: Coordinated outfits without a jacket, knitwear and softer construction, and collars for men.

Your guidelines could then follow each category for men and women and an example of when each type of clothing is appropriate. (E.g. Formal business dress is required in formal presentations and when meeting with a client.) Your guidelines can also include grooming.

If you are dealing with uniforms you will need to be even more specific than with regular dress, and stipulate type of jewelry, hem lengths, heel heights and color specifications. You will also need to document what not to wear!

Paste photographs of appropriate (and inappropriate) dress in each category on the bulletin board or an area devoted to the new look. Take photographs of employees in well-groomed examples of each level of business dress. Publish them in company newsletters, articles, and public displays. A picture tells a thousand words.

If the company has encountered many appearance challenges relating to diversity or religious issues, it would be wise to publish acceptable solutions to these issues in the dress code. For example, long hair or dreadlocks can be tied back or coiled, tattoos must be covered and visible body rings are to be removed at work.

Consistent appearance standards are important components of the corporate identity. If you are interested in working with companies on their branding and corporate image, your consulting skills will be called on to reinforce that

concept. Companies devote much of their budget to the image of their logo, interiors and their building and many person-hours to their advertising, marketing and mission. It is our job to remind them that the way their people act, speak, look and behave represent that mission on a consistent and sustainable basis, and we have the tools to help them.

<u>NOTES</u>*:*

Chapter 8

BUSINESS DEVELOPMENT

The evolution of a successful image consulting business

At first blush being in business is exciting! It is exhilarating to plan, anticipate and talk to everyone about starting a business. Businesses are organic, growing and evolving the whole time, but need constant attention, especially at the beginning. It is important to realize that a business goes through stages, often not in linear fashion, but in direct proportion to the amount of time and energy you put in. Each stage has its own set of challenges, but also its successes. Don't miss the success markers at every stage and be on the lookout for the lessons to be learned at each stage. Like "Groundhog Day," you cannot grow if you do not heed the lessons the universe is telling you at every bump in the road.

If you start your image consulting business, then go on vacation for a couple of weeks, look after a sick mother, attend a conference, decide you don't know enough and take some courses and spend time waiting for your materials to all be perfect and in place, your company will fall back to the stage or stages before, and you will wonder what happened.

Don't compare yourself to anyone else, but go through this chapter and be aware of the moments you are not doing what you need to do at each stage. You will notice that none of the actions demands an MBA or higher degree. Tell yourself the truth at all times and practice the power of NOW! If you make a plan and follow it, without a doubt you will naturally progress to the next stage of your business.

STAGE ONE

This stage is exciting and scary

You are defining who you are and what you offer. Friends and family are supportive and assure you that "Everybody will want your services," and "There's a huge market out there." Twenty years ago I was poised to become a major success, or so I thought. I knew my stuff, had a name for my company and services, had created marketing materials, and had lots of passion and enthusiasm. I had a launching party; I sent out a flyer to everyone and then sent another flyer to 1000 people in my real-estate friend's community. The return on a flyer is 1%-5%, right? I waited for the calls to roll in. And guess what happened next? Nothing! I didn't have one single call from the flyer and my friends all had great images because I had practiced on them while I was honing my skills. I was busy doing all the other four part time jobs (all image related) to pay rent, but they only camouflaged the fact that I really wasn't doing much for my own company. In addition, my marketing theories for a small image company needed a big revision. The lessons learned here were clear. I needed to establish a reputation in one community at a time individual-by-individual, group by group. I needed to speak personally to clubs, individuals, organizations, business people, college students, associations, and institutes. I had not set a target market because I wanted to work with everyone. Bad idea! I trudged through what Christina Ong; *AICI CIP President of ImageWorks, Asia* calls the Valley of Death. The VOD!

NOTES:

STAGE TWO

In this stage, the VOD gets deeper

You have worked and worked and put in your hours, done your action items for the week and have nothing in tangible clients or speaking engagements to show for it. Well, maybe that freebie client who wants you to speak to her Garden Club. Instead of "Oh, everybody needs you", your friends and family whom you haven't spoken to in weeks, are looking at you as though you have lost your mind and telling you through the locked door that you should really give it all up now. Your husband asks how much money you have made this week and you tell him weakly that you don't expect clients yet. Too early, you say airily. And, of course, you are having such fun.

You will be successful if you persist in the face of adversity and failure.

At this stage it is important to keep your word to yourself.

Plan your work and work your plan. No amount of justifications and excuses can substitute for doing what you said you would do when you said you would do it. You will start to trust yourself and develop the self-confidence it takes to run a business.

> **Stage Two Test #1:**
>
> *Do you make a realistic to-do list for the day or week and get everything on that list done?*

Stop distracting yourself

Yes, you read that right. Most of our distractions are self-imposed! Notice when you are going off track and bring yourself back. Be disciplined and avoid distractions like internet browsing, morning TV and soap operas, like the plague. You will be successful if you are very focused and plan for distractions before they eat you up.

> **Stage Two -Test #2:**
>
> *Are you always very busy and feeling overwhelmed?*
>
> *or*
>
> *Do you plan realistically what you are going to do that day and that week, glue your derriere to a seat and do it?*

Marketing is the critical activity at this stage. You simply will not have everything perfectly ready, even if you want to, because much of your work and your self-promotion practices will evolve as you do them. Set yourself tasks at the beginning of the week and complete them. There is a law of the universe that operates at this stage which cannot be ignored. The focused energy you put in at this point of your business is directly proportional to the results. But it is rarely one effort to one result. It is more like ten to one. In other words, if you make ten phone calls, only one will yield results. Most people give up too soon at this stage because their input is too small. Keep going, however bored, frustrated or tired you are, until you have that one result, even if it is tiny.

Network your tail off and join at least two different business network clubs or groups. Visit your local Chamber of Commerce events regularly. Get to know people in your city, academic, church and business communities. Decide on at least one target market and find out where those people hang out: churches, schools, colleges, trade associations and civic and town and country clubs for example. Offer to speak at events and gatherings where you will bump into them naturally. Marketing an image consulting business is very like marketing for a coach, therapist or counselor. People need to see you, trust you and speak to you before you have gained a word-of-mouth reputation.

Stop right now and write the names of three people you want to approach, or three groups you would like to target.

Organization	Name

Even if you have to find other streams of income, you still have your eye on that entrepreneurial freedom.

Stage Two – Test #3

Here is the test: Have you learned valuable lessons from at least three mistakes in the last six months?

What mistakes did you make, and what lessons did you learn? Stop now and record them.

Mistake	Lesson learned

STAGE THREE

Reach into Your Community and Get Support

At this point things are happening. The phone starts to ring. You have been playing and working to your maximum capacity. Work is now like a huge game for you, a full expression of your vision and the person you are designing yourself to be in the world. It lights you up and you would do it even if you were not being paid. Whatever you do: work, play, charitable activities, hobbies, grocery shopping or going to the dentist, you do it passionately. You have invented a vision that is much bigger than you are, and you live your entire life inside of that vision. Here's the test: Do you have energy to spare, even after you have worked your tail off?

> ### *Success at this stage is to work and play equally hard as if there were no difference.*

However, you still seem to be toiling, all by yourself at all hours and burning the midnight oil or up at dawn just to get it all done. Your family becomes a shadow cast that you hope will understand now you have turned into a recluse. You meet them at meals or bump into them in the bathroom. They have to drag you out of your cave to make Christmas dinner or come to the school play. At first you are convinced that you can't afford to have official employees, and that might be a wise financial decision as you look at the meager sums you brought in last month. To be honest, I was such a consummate do-it-yourself-er, I would not have even known how to use staff if they had banged on my door. However, at this stage you need help and there are ways to get help without spending the money you haven't got.

First, clearly distinguish what your most critical role is for your company. Are you needed for sales and marketing? Yes to start with, but no, sooner than you think. How about consultations and training? Yes, to start with. Do you need to do administration, wrap product packages for clients, run errands, do the bookkeeping, or accounting, and spend hours desktop publishing? No, not necessarily

Consider that you may be doing lots of these things to keep busy, and to stay firmly in your comfort zone! All this activity allows you to avoid doing the things that are critical to moving forward. I noticed that I was always monumentally busy, but brought in so little money I was working for about ten dollars an hour and sometimes below minimum wage. Be honest about the hours you put in for each activity. With those statistics you can now plan the areas of your business that can use help. How can you get good solid help that actually costs you little to no money?

Use the worksheet on the next page to capture your thoughts.

Activity	*Hours Required*	*Cost per Hour*

You can go to colleges and find out about intern programs. College students will often do three- month sessions, (or longer if you work it out), not for pay but for college credit. Draw up a clear job description with set hours per day or per week and give clear parameters, just like any job. The college might also have a set of forms for you and the intern to fill out every week. Be prepared to mentor and coach the student. Rather than a chore or a waste of time, consider that this will strengthen your own practices. I have found that the relationship is largely a matter of trial and error in the first month or so, but while they are keen and learning the job, be sure to set out ground rules. When I

think back, every upset has been caused by miscommunication on my part or not adequately stating what I expected. Your aim is to be able to go away on vacation or attend a conference, or leave your business for a short while without disaster or a downturn in productivity.

Develop a large network of support with other experts. An image consultant is a resource person. We must have a stable of people to whom we can refer our clients if we can't do the job, and with whom we can work. Our resources help expand our business, often for free! You can work out a commission or referral fee; or simple refer the work to them with no financial attachments. You can also barter services. An easy example is to think of your hairdresser and colorist as experts in your company. Choose them wisely for their technical expertise and their communication skills. Both are vital. If you send them clients on a consistent basis, they might consider bartering their services or at least giving you a discount for your own haircuts and color.

I used to work a lot with women who sold direct designer collections such as Doncaster, Carlisle, Juliana Collezione, Worth, and others. If I brought clients to their homes or studios, we worked out a commission, and I selected clothes as payment! The designer's local representative would be only too anxious to dress me in their company's image, and at the beginning of my career for many of the leaner years, I remember having no extra cash but stepping out in gorgeous designer wear, looking affluent and successful. Image is everything!

I also bartered services that could be done as short-term projects such as desktop publishing and workbook design, with experts who needed image services, communication coaching, or branding work. We usually worked out a retail-to-retail cost or a similar hour for

hour fee. If you write everything out (and I mean every detail) upfront, these exchanges can be very successful. If you leave things to chance or rely on the looser practices of casual friendship, you are leaving yourself wide open to disaster.

Another way you can use your community is to form or join mastermind groups, leads clubs, community or business groups who can be your word-of-mouth marketing teams. Your business will expand in direct proportion to the number of people who are telling your community about you. The lasting relationships that you forge at this point are the ones built on trust. You could also barter or discount your services to anyone in this close circle of influence, because you want them to be out there representing you *and* looking good. I joined a leads club at the beginning of my career (after the flyer failure) and did makeovers on at least 75% of the women in the club. To this day, many of them are still in my support group: my lawyer, insurance agent, financial advisor, flower and interior designer, and health and nutritional consultant.

Group	Client / Colleague	Service

Employ your family. They are your greatest support system and are the most long-suffering members of your circle of influence. They also have wonderful skills if you can tap into them without exploiting the labor force. In the early 1990's my then teenaged daughter, Alexandra was the only person I knew in the house who could type. She typed everything for me and was paid an hourly fee for her work, which in turn gave her pocket money. She will insist to this day that she was a victim of slave labor, and the work arrested her development, but I did notice that she can type like the wind and her administrative skills got her handsomely through college! Kids love knowing that they hold the secrets of the internet in their hands-and you don't: Think of the transference of power!

My husband, Frank is always a marvellous resource for knotty business decisions and is a calm, dispassionate consultant with whom to toss over growth ideas. He is wonderful at proofing, clarifying sentences and thoughts and taking an idea into the future to see its viability. The thing I am most grateful to him for, is that he knows I have to constantly replenish myself, and he is always supportive of the extra-curricular education and the extensive travel that I do. If I finally admit that I am tired and say the kitchen is closed tonight and the chef is off, he will take me out to dinner. That kind of support is invaluable to an entrepreneur.

The trick is to make firm dates with your family and keep them. Take them to dinner to celebrate your successes or help overcome your bad times. Pay special attention to your children. Share with them everything that's going on, because in doing so you are actually training a new generation in entrepreneurial and leadership skills. If you think they won't understand, consider that you are actually demeaning the relationship and curbing their growth. Even if it's not obvious, they will be especially vigilant of the way you overcome your upsets and handle adverse situations. They grow and learn, seemingly by osmosis. Acknowledge their support loudly and regularly. A great way to do that is sit down with them at an Appreciation and Acknowledgement dinner every week so you get an opportunity to become a Mom or Dad once again and show how much you value their support.

Acknowledge yourself as the precious source of your business.

If you are in a business called "*Me Inc.,*" you are successful if you constantly renew yourself, physically, creatively, spiritually and psychologically. You can't always be brilliant or vital, sane or creative if you go on and on relying on yourself for council. Appraise the activities in your life for balance and reach outside yourself for powerful renewal. Take good care of the Golden Goose and look after body, mind and soul. Here is the test: Do you love and adore yourself and the life you live?

Manage your cash flow.

In business cash is king! You are successful if you know where the next inflow of cash will come from and manage your marketing efforts and expenses accordingly. I have known people who have tons of money and get big contracts but they were so poor at managing cash and overspent when times were good, that they became heavily in credit card debt. Our business is often feast or famine, so plan for the lean times. Here is the test: Do you make a marketing, networking and cash flow plan for every quarter?

Walk the talk as an image consultant.

You are successful if you are "whole and complete." By that, I mean you have a high level of integrity. If you say you will do or portray something that people expect, you need to deliver. If you don't, keep cleaning up any mishaps as an ongoing practice, even if it's scary. You will not only be a successful businessperson but also someone whom people respect everywhere. You are successful if all you do is to operate from solid, ethical business practices and demand them of others.

Stage Three - Test #4:

Do you have upsets that need to be cleaned up with anybody at all?

STAGE FOUR

You have made a ton of mistakes and come through it all with the battle scars to show for it, and a stronger, more resilient attitude. This is the stage when you can predict how you and your clients or potential clients will behave. You will have evolved new services and dropped a few of the old ways of doing things that do not work. You will let go pain-in-the-neck clients, raise your fees and possibly hire a full time administrative or marketing person. You may even have a team. Your resource circle is evolving and growing as is your support group.

Be a resounding "Yes" to opportunities

At this stage, you see an opportunity and do not shrink from it because you are afraid to make a mistake. You now know that you learn from your shortfalls, risks and challenges, so take on assignments that may be a stretch for you. Invent opportunities. You will be successful if you take risks, and not if you play it safe all the time. Contribute freely to your communities without expecting a "quid pro quo." The opportunity here is to learn an enormous amount and transfer all those skills to your business.

Stage Four – Test #1

Have you planned one stretch goal or challenging activity for the next three months?

It is important at this stage to turn your back on anyone in your circle who is sabotaging your success. However painful, release the naysayers, the pessimists, the controllers, the hangers-on and the drones who do not pull their weight. It is now time to take on a larger vision, greater challenges, larger accounts, and longer term consulting, training or coaching. Everyone around you needs to be inspired by your vision and leadership. Don't be afraid to say no to the smaller stuff, or yes to a big account, and not know how to do it. The challenge at this stage is to stop getting bored, complacent or arrogant.

You will revise your practices and people will be asking your opinion. Your marketing will be more sophisticated and your web site will need revamping, to represent the company you have now become. You have created your own materials and have your own ideas; you have now outgrown the masters you trained with. You will now be able to go to branding classes and relate what they are saying to your own company. Your brand has emerged. I am not suggesting that you can't create a brand in the early stages of a company. Far from it! However at Stage 4, your brand is now solidifying and becoming an authentic representation of your experience, values, training, services and failures. It is yours through and through from blood, sweat and tears.

At this stage, you are successful if you know the difference you make and charge accordingly

At this stage, your vision is less about you and more towards the world. Your community makes demands on you because you are so good at what you do; they won't let you **not** do it. Don't undervalue your contribution. We think of success as an individual thing but actually people are empowered in some way by being around you, so success is more like sunlight flooding a dark room and everyone gets the benefit. At this stage you shed light into the lives of everyone around you. Here is the test: How are the people around you doing? Are they flourishing?

STAGE FIVE

The final stage is mentoring. You are now in a position to write the book; train others around you so that they can replace you; create new and innovative techniques, and be a force in the industry. You are a master at the services you provide and only take on what you love. You have delegated your other services to your support team. You may be the keynote at the conferences but more than likely, your trainees will be the luminaries. The smart, bright, young things seem to have taken over, but your vision includes succession planning. You are no longer threatened by them as smarter, brighter, younger, or better looking. Like your children, they are the ones who will take your work over and become better at it. It's all in the plan for the evolution of your company and life itself. You now can give yourself away with grace and ease and watch others grow, knowing that you have left a secure legacy. It's time for you to move on to your next adventure.

HOW TO KEEP YOUR GOALS BLOOMING

It may come as no surprise to you that resolutions, good ideas and goals have a shelf life of about 1 day! Somehow the next day, your resolve weakens, you start to regret having made the promise and you forget entirely what caused the excitement in the first place. Sound familiar? Here are a few ideas to keep the excitement in place.

Invent a vision for the goal that lights you up

The goal will then be simply a means to an exciting end. The vision is the inspiration that drives the project. For example, "I have to lose 20 lbs by March 31st" might lose some rapture the minute you feel deprived of food. "A health program to create an abundance of energy, beauty and vitality" or "Unleashing the Goddess Within Me" might get you farther along.

Start with the end in mind

Establish a date by when the goal will be accomplished and work backwards. Even more than that, write out the result of your outcomes. If you envision the end result it will add spice and flavor to the goal. If it doesn't get you out of bed in the morning, why are you taking it on? Olympic running champions were interviewed and asked what they were thinking at the start and throughout the race. They all said that they envisioned themselves crossing the finish line in victory.

Goals need to be SMART

That means Specific, Measurable, Attainable, Realistic (or Written) and Timed. Lacking any one of those ingredients and they will wilt and die before their time, and you will wonder why.

Organize your physical and mental work- space

Work on distractions as they come up. Take a look at what you let interfere with your work and reorganize your environment or your time management to let time and space flow. Do not create walls and barriers to creativity. Get rid of clutter; clean your calendar and your work place at the end of every day. Start every day fresh and free of baggage. Clear up broken agreements, phone calls not made and actions not taken every day. Work on one thing at a time!

Get the plan out of your head and make it into a physical object

Left as a thought, the goal will languish and be forgotten in the morass of your memory. Nothing personal, but we all have memory-mush between our ears. Studies have shown that short-term memory can only hold about seven things at once. (George A. Miller, "The Magical Number Seven, Psychology Review (March 1956), vol.63, no 2.) Make your goals into projects and house them in separate files. Then select funny, witty or appropriate pictures to decorate your file. You could also use pretty paper or a colorful file to hold the written plan. Make the physical existence of your project fun and beautiful to behold. You will be amazed at the difference it makes to reach for a work of art, rather than a manila folder! Transfer all the actions into your day timer, palm pilot or something you can refer to on a daily basis. By the way, a computer is fine to house your projects but it does not have the emotional or aesthetic attraction of color, pictures or attractive paper. Carry a little notebook or some form of satellite tool with you at all times to capture those brilliant ideas you have while driving.

Build a bridge over troubled waters

An action plan to fulfill a goal needs to alter the flow of life. If it doesn't, you will soon know because the flow of life will be like a huge hurricane and flood the plans.

"The reasonable man adapts himself to the conditions that surround him. The unreasonable man adapts the surrounding conditions to himself. All progress depends on the unreasonable man."

George Bernard Shaw

Bolster the plan and the actions towards the goal with practices and procedures that will make it happen. Write a list of actions you will do that day. Do nothing else but those actions. For example, if you are writing a proposal, do not open e-mail, answer the phone for 2 hours or make phone calls. Close the door on interruptions until you have finished it!

Forgetting is useful

We sometimes forget to do something and we also make mistakes. Those are good reminders! Why? Because they are forceful wake-up calls to put in a stronger structure or more structures to make it happen. Ask yourself, why did I forget? Why did that not work the way I

had intended it to? What is needed to make this happen? But keep going, having learned a useful lesson. Don't waste time blaming yourself and others and don't let anything stop you.

Make someone the steward of your goals

Left to our own devices, especially as entrepreneurs, if we do not do what we set out to do, we have a tendency to put a guilt trip on ourselves or let ourselves get away with it. Both are unproductive strategies. Get a coach, mentor or buddy for the project and report in daily or weekly. My buddy and I have been the keeper of each other's weekly goals for many years now. The practice acts like a refresh button on my computer. At the end of each week, we say what we did and did not accomplish, thereby completing the week, so that we can start the next week fresh to recommit.

Be your own public relations machine

Keep telling people about your ideas and promote the successes. Ask people to support you in your project. I have noticed that people are particularly bad about supporting someone on a diet. They never think they are serious and urge them to go off it for the occasion and that it will never hurt! That is not support, that's sabotage! Watch out for the Naysayers. Make your goals real and valid by reporting on the victories and even the breakdowns. The more you broadcast your progress and ask for ideas from everyone, the more the outcomes will seem real to you and everyone else too.

Have fun

Have fun by setting up rules and games for yourself. A colleague of mine in sales has a game that he plays to count the number of "no's" he gets to complete the sale. He has found out that he needs about eight no's for every "yes" he gets. That way, a "no" doesn't seem so bad, just a stepping stone to yes! Notice and celebrate your victories, however small. If you aren't enthusiastic about your project and even your failures and mistakes, go back and invent another vision.

Consistency is Key

How are your project goals doing? Have you completed some, abandoned others? A really useful exercise is to look back and see why some were accomplished and others were not. What were the ingredients in the goals that survived to fruition? What was missing in the way you approached goals that didn't make it? Now don't all rush and say "time" or "money" because as you and I know, those are both self-imposed smoke screens dedicated to keep our comfort level in place.

If the monkeys on your shoulders were chattering loudly you forgot that you didn't have to listen! Take a look at the structures you used to keep the goals in place. Were they sufficient to get the job done? At least one of those structures was to accept and welcome those monkeys, let them quietly slip off your shoulders or punch them in the nose! "Thanks for sharing, but adios." Some of your goals needed extra time and some less. Those are also valuable lessons to learn.

Celebrate the goals that did succeed, and give yourself a raise.

Award and reward yourself for a job well done. Remember you are the boss and the employee. So be a compassionate boss. Don't let yourself off the hook, but give yourself a break also.

This excerpt from the book: *The Way of Transformation* by **Karlfried Graf von Durckheim** is compelling. He describes the ability to accept and welcome our demons, rather than trying to protect ourselves from their inevitable force, which only keeps them in place.

> *The man who...falls upon hard times in the world will not, as a consequence, turn to that friend who offers him refuge and comfort and encourages his old self to survive. Rather he will seek out someone who will faithfully and inexorably help him to risk himself, so that he may endure the suffering and pass courageously through it, thus making of it a "raft that leads to the shore." Only to the extent that man exposes himself over and over again to annihilation, can that which is indestructible arise within him. In this lies the dignity of daring. Thus the aim of practice is not to develop an attitude which allows man to acquire a state of harmony and peace wherein nothing can trouble him....*
>
> *The first necessity is that we should have the courage to face life and to encounter all that is most perilous in the world.*

Chapter 9

CREATING YOUR BRAND

Are you a brand or a commodity?

Branding has become a global concept. A brand transcends borders and epitomizes universal human values. A brand appeals to us from emotional, physical, psychological and rational standpoints. It reaches into our soul and touches our deep-seated dreams and aspirations. Then it fulfills the expectation that we have barely dared express.

Think of "Just Do It!"

Unless we have a marketing strategy and we identify our unique quality, we do not have a competitive edge in the marketplace! We need to know who we are and why we are different, otherwise we will just sound like everyone else. In the economic fluctuations of our time, there are millions of consultants trying to make a living. Anyone with "consultant" or "coach" in the title is particularly vulnerable to being and sounding generic. Do you want to be another "me-too" company, writing organizational jargon, irrelevant to the lives of the clients you want to attract?

How can we persuade others to use our services unless we define what makes us special? We need to find attributes not easily emulated by our competitors, define the benefits of our services and provide the expectation of a promise we can deliver that withstands the test of time. Do people even know what an image consultant or professional development consultant is or does? What can you do to differentiate yourself from other image consultants, in-store personal shoppers, makeup artists, colorists, stylists and hairstylists? What can you do to brand your company? Successful image consulting companies have a brand, a distinguishable edge that overrides any issues, concerns, or upsets that arise, and gets attention in an increasingly crowded marketplace.

HOW IMAGE INFLUENCES PERCEPTION

Clearly, human beings make judgments about each other based purely on the way we look, act, speak, and behave. Image consultants in particular are under considerable scrutiny! The minute we announce ourselves as an Image Consultant, we have set ourselves up! Potential clients look at us differently and wonder whether they can trust us with their most cherished possession: their image! They evaluate us on a scale of attractiveness, whether they consider us credible professionals, friend or foe, and worthy of their time. They code all the information into their personal experience computer and start making evaluations about our intellect, social status, character, temperament, and professional abilities.

Since the initial split-second contact with people is eye-to-body, they look at clothes before face. Since human beings make profound value judgments from superficial evidence, it would seem important to choose carefully the way we dress and take conscious control of our appearance, communication,

personal and professional practices, and habits purely to communicate the messages we intend to represent.

An important consideration is to dress at the same high standard all the time. If people react positively to our appearance and presence each time they see us, they will also build up a level of trust in our performance in other areas, such as our work skills, intelligence, capabilities, and competence. On the other hand, if our image communicates mixed messages, we run the risk of negative opinions quite unrelated to the skills and capabilities we actually possess.

Our Own Image

Looking good is important for our business. Being effective starts with looking and feeling good. Personal appearance, body language, etiquette, business practices, presentation and communication are important elements of image which we teach and are fun to learn. It is definitely worth our while to achieve that extra polish and the quality look that not only gives us self-confidence but also gives our clients a sense that we are walking the talk. Our image needs to say that we are consistent with our message:

- Effective
- Caring
- Professional
- Considerate
- Pulled together
- Current
- Efficient
- Trustworthy
- Harmonious
- Attending to detail
- Impeccable
- Likeable
- Having wide appeal

Consistency of Image

The definition of "Professionalism" in any field, from Olympic Ice Skating to Corporate Executive Officer might be:

- A high standard of performance

- Consistency of performance

Similarly, in the area of appearance we are perceived as professional if we have:

> ### A standard below which we will not fall.
>
> *Lynne Marks*

After all, our appearance is our most visible possession and speaks loudest. Business associates cannot see our Mercedes parked outside or our gorgeous home, so our style and preferences are judged by our appearance alone.

We need to be responsible that our business image:

- Provides instant clout

- Makes us look credible, stable and friendly

- Projects feminine and attractive, or masculine and clean cut

- Represents our personal and professional accomplishments

- Is consistent with our vision, values and stand in life

The assessments one person may have of another are not purely based on appearance. We are also judged by the way we speak. Vocabulary, accent, grammar, length of sentence, and articulation all express, in incredibly subtle ways, our education, financial, geographical, and social backgrounds. Appearance, body language, and nonverbal practices are all interpreted with equal significance.

The second aspect of consistency of appearance is equally important. We as entrepreneurs invest considerable sums in our web sites, logo and printed material. We sometimes forget that our image needs to be consistent with our message. An overgrown hairstyle and black roots just do not cut it for our image! It is just as important for us to invest in our appearance as our business cards. Image is even more a component of our total brand than it is for our clients.

Why Image Is Important To Your Brand.

When your image is of a consistently high standard, you project a sharper message of:

- Quality
- Responsibility
- Success

You have more self-confidence and a heightened responsiveness to and by clients and work associates, represent your product more effectively, and give yourself a significant advantage in the marketplace

You become more service oriented if your image is handled and therefore, able to switch the attention from yourself and on to the needs of your clients.

You enhance your potential for professional growth and promotion. You embody a valuable part of your brand.

Is your image consistent on a day-to-day basis with:

- Your corporate identity and brand?

- Your environment; house, car, the objects around you?

- Your professional skills and talents?

- Your vision, values, mission, and goals in life?

- Your nonverbal and verbal communication?

What car would you choose for your company image?

Touch points

Whenever your company or any representation of your brand touches the public, it and you will make an impression, conscious or not, in the minds and emotions of the public. These are touch points with the public and all have to reflect the value and essence of your brand.

Every single thing about your brand has to express and ensure brand value.

All the tangible and intangible elements have to be dissected and reinvented to be consistent. Every single touch to your client must provide the same experience. What are people saying about their experience of you, your appearance, your professionalism and your service when you are not there? Are your clients surprised at the value you give? Are they empowered and in action? Did they feel comfortable enough to ask the silly and embarrassing questions? Did your service leave them wanting more, feeling proud and worthwhile and did it improve their stature in the world?

Are your materials and products also consistent with your brand values?

Values

Good branding starts with research, identifying the image of your company, the problems that must be addressed by that image, and the way your customers perceive your organization now and in the future.

What are the universal **values** that you stand for and are the underpinnings of your brand?

> ***At London Image Institute, our values are <u>courage</u>, <u>freedom</u>, self-expression, and <u>beauty</u>. What we stand for in life is the courage to develop yourself and become the quintessential version of your ultimate vision of yourself, and even beyond that, for others you train.***

Our commitment to you is that this is what you get when you are trained by us. We have made this into our vision statement:

> ***By 2030, all people will have the courage and freedom to flourish."***

What can we count on *you* for? These values are not what you aspire to be, or strengths compared to weaknesses, or even personality traits. These values are in your DNA! Ask your clients and everyone around you who you are. Frequently, if you think back to what you value about your parents, those are your values too.

Banner

Articulate your vision or brand promise into a single bold statement that is the slogan or the banner that goes before you into battle. It epitomizes what you stand for in powerful, everyday language. For our Institute we promise: Bold, Charismatic Leaders who Dare to Make a Difference." As for our individuals, we make you look "Taller, Richer, Thinner, Younger, Sexier!" Put the slogan everywhere in your materials and your brochures. Use it as a tag line after your company name, or when you use your elevator statement. Let it engulf and use you.

Which famous brands do these statements represent?

"When you care to send the very best."

_____

"Just do it.

_____

"The relentless pursuit of perfection."

_____

"We create magic moments in the lives of families."

_____

yensiD, suxeL, ekiN, kramllaH

Defining a Brand:

1. The consistent experience people have of you based on your values, formal and informal contribution, performance, manners, visual, verbal, and nonverbal messages, your vision and stand for the world.

2. Your unique qualities and appearance that set you apart and allow you to stand out from the crowd.

3. A way of differentiating yourself from your competition.

The Soul of the Brand

If you distilled what your company stands for into one or two words, what would that be? Volvo is "safety', Coca-Cola is "vitality", Virgin is the "people's champion", Nike was "hero" (then it got confused!) Timberland's products "only get better with age." London Image Institute is "People Flourishing".

Personality of the Brand

What is the personality of your brand- e.g. Lover, Outlaw, Hero, Explorer? Columbia Sportswear for example, used the tough, mother image of its owner to represent that its skiwear and boots are resilient and like her, never wear out. Land Rover aficionados are "form follows function" fans, representing the rugged explorer who dislikes the frivolous and values a vehicle built to last. We at London Image Institute used a lion to portray strength, power, professionalism and King of the Jungle!

If you were to pick a spokesperson for your company, who would that be and why?

_____

_____

Your brand might take on a personality all its own and you might be surprised to find out it is not necessarily like you. It might even be an affectionate cartoon character. Think about your target market and the people you are attracting. This will give you some insight into the personality your brand is currently projecting. Is it consistent with your intention and your message?

Yes_____ No_____

Do you appeal to the executive who has no time?

Yes_____ No_____

If you are simplifying his life, providing cost and time saving solutions, and transforming him into the sleek, well-organized manager of life he has always wanted to be, pink and purple flowers on your letterhead are not going to cut it with him!

> *Philosophy:*
> *A series of beliefs that*
> *benefit the customer.*

Give your target markets a reason to buy from you. (Rational). How do your products and services make them feel? (Emotional). How does the service or product work? Is it easy or complex? Are you simplifying and enhancing their lives? (Physical).

Iconography

What are the forms, shapes, materials, colors and type styles of your brand?

_____

_____

Are these expressed in your logo, printed material, website layout, illustrations, and photographs? If you are not graphically inclined, get help with this from an expert. Describe your brand values, essence, and banner to a graphic artist and let him come up with some examples. Do they excite and inspire you and represent the freshness and energy you put into your business? Brands are never wallpaper that fades into the background. They are always current, trustworthy and engage an emotion such as joy, elegance, or confidence; they are never faddish or insignificant.

Appeal

Does your font, shape of typeface, logo, and choice of colors appeal to both men and women?

Yes_____ No_____

Sometimes your women clients have male tastes in graphics, so do not restrict yourself to a very feminine look. Match the look of the logo and font to your brand essence, not your existing clientele. Is there an exciting energy and tension in your colors such as red, black and white or a calm and elegance as in gray and silver? What is the *tone of voice* in your brochure and your website? A font with a serif will be read slower than sans serif typefaces. If you want to denote speed and energy, you will use a font without serifs. If you want to portray elegance and leisure, use serifs.

Inspiration

What is the source of inspiration for your brand?

_____

_____

Is it artistic, high tech, humanistic, classic, pillar of society, iconoclastic, educational, witty, humorous, or a few of these?

_____

_____

Think about your values and let your platform or context speak for you. Target, a maverick general merchandising store in the U.S. representing "Urban Chic" for example, used Pop Art with multiple photographs like an Andy Warhol painting to illustrate their ordinary house wares in an "Expect More. Pay Less" campaign. They have branded the whole store as a design-forward, urban-chic concept and their advertisements are always astonishing. The famous visual wit in the Absolut campaign has brought the brand to be the #1 vodka in the US and in the top 100 list of global brands.

Infrastructure

Are you a House of Brands or a Branded House?

_____

_____

Are you carrying several names under your own brand?

_____

_____

If you have a well-known makeup or jewelry line for example, are you giving away or diluting your brand to another company? If you have a few brands under your umbrella you might want to pull them all together and project yourself as *the* brand. It is more powerful to harness all your brands under one concept. Co-branding with AICI is also a smart move, so that you have the credibility of a larger association behind you.

> **Remember...**
>
> **As an image consultant, you are the walking, talking representation of your brand! People, companies, and even countries have brands. Are you clear what yours is?**

Be consistent. Use the same artwork each time your logo or slogan is reproduced and always use the exact same colors. Put guidelines for logo usage in writing. If you ever hire interns or assistants, consider developing a policy and procedure manual, and job descriptions to ensure that customer service and product or service performances are of consistently high quality.

Brand Promise

As in those examples, your philosophy is a series of beliefs that benefit the customer, compounded into one word, banner, or phrase.

Your brand should be projected on everything you print, advertise, say, and do. Use your logo or tagline on stationery, envelops, invoices, cards, signage, web sites, advertising, brochures, give-away items, etc.

Keep in mind that every experience a customer or potential customer has with your business, including phone calls, service calls, and product performance, must reinforce and support your image.

What Every Branded Woman Should Know	
That punctuality speaks louder than your clothes	Clear, succinct communication
How to speak in public	How to tell one on yourself
How to use personal space to your best advantage	Matching people's energy level
Steady eye contact, a smile which hits the eyes and a good handshake	That listening makes you more intelligent and compassionate than talking.
Showing genuine curiosity for the people you meet	The right spot to hem sleeves
The colors that you cannot wear	How to say no graciously
How to buy pants that fit	Never show your underwear
Your natural balance points	How to develop a capsule wardrobe
Never use frosted or white eye shadows, frosted lipsticks or high shine eye-liner over the age of 13	How to blend your makeup
The cost-per-wear of all your major clothes	When to arrive, when to leave and what to bring
How to create a style	How to get out of the potted plants when networking
How to write a thank you note	How to describe your background and experience in under two minutes
A 30-second self-promotion statement without sounding full of yourself	Knowing what you stand for in life
A 5-20 minute workout	How your strengths contribute to a team
Current events	Saying what you need to say to a man without getting emotional
How to put people at ease	How to balance your life with fun and play
How to balance your check book	That acknowledging friends, family or coworkers will instantly enhance the relationship.
Saying "I apologize" is amazingly attractive	That acknowledging friends, family or coworkers will instantly enhance the relationship
Chatting loudly on your cell phone in public is as attractive as chewing gum with your mouth open	Doing what you said you would do, no matter what

What Every Branded Woman Should Have	
The perfect jacket for every occasion	A closet of 100% WOW clothes
A confident stance, walk, and posture	An elegant tote or feminine briefcase that goes with everything
A subscription to the Wall Street Journal	A pair of good sunglasses
A personal vision and mission statement	A clothing steamer
A sharp black or taupe pant suit to pack for a business trip	Well fitting underwear
Great denim or black jeans that shave off 5 lbs.	Good business cards and stationary
A well designed haircut	Health and Auto insurance
Hair color that matches your skin tone	Humility
A great alterations person or tailor	A fantastic attitude
Excellent neutral makeup and skincare products	A wonderful set of jewelry
Credit	A wonderful set of jewelry that goes that goes with everything
Wonderful black plants	At least one pair of elegant, well-heeled shoes
Great guy friends to escort you to events (if single)	A purse too small to carry the kitchen sink
A fail-safe day timer or PDA which contains your life and your brain	

What Every Branded Man Should Know

That punctuality speaks louder than your tie	Clear, succinct communication
How to speak in public	How to tell one on yourself
How to use personal space to your best advantage	How to match people's energy level
Steady eye contact, a smile which hits the eyes and a good handshake	That listening makes you more intelligent and compassionate than talking.
Showing genuine curiosity for the people you meet	How to build a capsule wardrobe
The colors that you can wear	The cost-per-wear of all your major clothes
When to arrive, when to leave and what to bring	How to write a thank you note
How to work a room	Current events
A 30-second self-promotion statement without sounding full of yourself	How to describe your background and experience in under two minutes
A 5-20 minute workout	How to put people at ease
How to balance your check book	Saying "I apologize" is amazingly attractive
That acknowledging friends, family or coworkers will instantly enhance the relationship	Chatting loudly on your cell phone in public is as attractive as chewing gum with your mouth open
Doing what you said you would do, by when you said you would do it no debate	The name of an impeccable tailor
How to tie a Windsor knot	Clean jokes
The difference between Worsted, Shetland & Lambs wool	The phone number of at least two wonderful restaurants
The colors that you can't wear, and suit designers that you can	Not to chew gum in public
The names of at least three great wines	If you don't wear something for a year give it to charity
A personal vision statement	How to cook three good meals
The European equivalents of your sizes	Your mate's important sizes
That you are supposed to go through a revolving door before she does	How to sew on a button
The names of a dozen flowers and a florist that will deliver them	That you never read a newspaper or eat anything while wearing suede
CPR	The only woman that will love you unconditionally is your mother
How to make friends with children	How to spit shine a pair of shoes
The name of the person who does your laundry	The name of the person who does your laundry

What Every Branded Man Should Know	
A 10-20 minute hotel workout	The shape of your face
Effective skincare products	That style is different from fashion
Wearing T-shirts under shirts can prolong their life	How to speak to any woman with respect
How to ask for directions	Doing complete work

What Every Branded Man Should Have	
Beautiful note cards	A single-breasted black or navy wool crepe suit, which is the first thing to pack for a business trip
A gorgeous blazer or sports coat	A Cashmere sweater
A great leather belt with a sterling or gold buckle	Incredibly well cut slacks
Black jeans	A good umbrella
A simple but great cookbook	A leather or suede jacket
An up-to-date passport	Great skincare products
Dress shirts not made of oxford cloth and not button-down collars	A lint brush
Shoe cleaning kit	A topcoat or Burberry that comes below the knees
A hand mirror	Two black crew or mock turtlenecks of different weights in silk, wool and cotton
A dictionary	A pair of sharp sunglasses
Photos of loved ones	Enough underwear and socks to last two weeks
A clothing steamer	Collar stays
A subscription to Consumer Report	Credit
A confident walk and posture	A subscription to the Wall Street Journal
A mission statement	A well designed haircut
A great alteration person or tailor	A fail-safe day-timer or PDA that contains your life and your brains
An elegant briefcase that goes with everything	Good quality business cards and stationary
Health and Auto insurance	Humility
A signet or wedding ring, not a college ring	A fantastic attitude
An elegant watch	A great pair of dress shoes
Bi-annual dental checkups	Deodorant and antiperspirant

Chapter 10

MARKETING

Small minds discuss people
Average minds discuss events
Great minds discuss ideas
Phenomenal minds create and
generate new language, ideas, and
events!

It is time to plan your marketing. The only way to accelerate your business is to accelerate your marketing. Don't pin all your hopes on one brochure, your new website or a single strategy. You will do a combination of networking, some cold calling, going to more leads groups, deepening the relationship with existing clients, creating new strategic alliances and creating exciting new ways to say the same thing! Remember, we are still in a look-good/feel good era, when millions of people from the thirty-something's to the baby-boomers have money to spend. Your marketing should include two thrusts:

1. Attraction Marketing when you show up everywhere.

2. Proactive, when you make the first moves and reach out into your community.

Who is your client and when do you know you are speaking to "the one?" Similar to the branding of your company, you need to create the profile of your "bull's eye" lead. You may of course have several target markets but each profile must be lovingly created as though these people were your best friends and you know everything that makes them exist, love, laugh and all their preferences.

Consider and answer these questions to guide your inquiry into a target market:

Who are they?

_____

What do they do?

_____

What is their age range?

_____

What is their income range?

_____

What level are they in their career?

_____

Do they have children, a spouse or are they single?

_____

What discretionary income might they have?

_____

What discretionary time might they have?

_____

What clothes or designers do they:

a) know? _____

b) buy? _____

What do they do in their spare time?

_____

_____

What other services do they use?

_____

What do they spend on hair color and cut?

_____

What are their needs?

_____

What are their complaints?

_____

How are you uniquely qualified to solve their problems?

_____

_____

_____

_____

What will happen if they do not solve their issues?

_____

_____

_____

When you have all this information, you are in a position to design your marketing activities. Remember, "People don't care how much I know until they know how much I care."

HOW TO ATTRACT CLIENTS

Be Charismatic.

One dictionary definition of Charisma is the "exceptional ability to give and receive". We often forget the *receive* bit. Charismatic people are the ones who attract others to them. They may not necessarily be good orators or embody the traditional notion of a leader but people want to be like them. They seem to be internally at peace and they inspire others to feel great about themselves.

Show up at community events

Join or start another leads group, attend Chamber events like "Eggs and Issues" and "After-Hours" parties. Make sure you are looking impeccable and walk the talk. Meet someone and then introduce that person to the next. Become the host of the event instead of the victim stuck by the potted plant. Ask questions and demonstrate genuine curiosity about the answers.

Exude self-confidence

EVERYONE wants self-confidence. That's what we are selling! And they can only gain self-confidence if they trust you enough to give it to themselves. Give short, free speeches to people who will want to see you before they trust you.

Listen!

When you want to discover anything about anyone JUST LISTEN. Have you ever put the radio in your head on loudspeaker? Louder and more persuasive than anything we are listening to at the time, it constantly blasts away in our head largely unnoticed .We might think we are listening to the conversation, but in fact we find ourselves simply waiting for others to finish in order to insert a choice morsel from our infinite wisdom or voice an opinion! Keen listening is an art and reflective listening is key. Say back to someone what he has just said to you, without sounding like a parrot and you will be considered more intelligent and more compassionate. If we *listen* with energy and passion for that person's energy and passion, we will hear what they want and need, and guess what, so will they! Then we can step in with a service that will help them gain confidence.

At your next networking meeting, speak in terms of benefits and give people examples they can identify with, rather than rattling on about your services and how you perform them. Ask questions until your companion *knows* you care and it becomes clear she needs this service of yours.

Be open to the suggestions of others and ASK FOR HELP! People love to feel they are making a contribution to YOU!

Be a Connector

Hold fun events that you can invite potential clients and their friends to. Dominique Isbecque, AICI, CIP, my co-author in the book: "*The Perfect Fit, How to Start an Image Consulting Business*" used to invite friends and clients to "Swap and Shop" events in her studio. She would promote closet clearings in advance and invite clients to bring their discarded items to the Swap and Shop. Customers paid in cash or swapped with other items. The fun was mixing, matching, exchanging and selling! She created a non-threatening way to introduce her services to potential clients. Any unwanted items were donated to charity.

Janet Morehead, owner of Mojo Maker has great services for singles. Single men and women meet separately at a

clothing store or boutique and they participate in the following:

- Create what vibe to they want to give out!

- Pick out an outfit for the night with the wardrobe consultants there to help them with their selection, using their Mojo Vibe as a Guide

- Guys: Get their hair touched-up by a hair stylist and moisturizer on their face.

- Girls: Get their hair touched up by a hair stylist and their makeup touched up by a makeup artist.

- Attend a Mini Flirting workshop where they learn the Mojo techniques and practice before the rendezvous with the opposite sex!

Then they head over with their new look to a bar where they get to show off their new look and practice their flirting techniques on each other. They play mingling games and give away prizes!!

Carla Harris, president of Heaven Sent Consultants created Martinis and Makeovers for her clients and friends of clients. She sold makeup in a fun-filled party atmosphere!

Joanne Rae, from VA has a fabulous marketing idea, especially good when you are just starting out. She is part of a women's mastermind group and for practice did individual consultations on all the women. Then her coach asked the group to write testimonials and helped her compose and collect them. Not only are they extraordinary letters that she can use for her brochure, but also Joanne reported an enormous increase in her self-confidence knowing what a difference she has made in the lives of all these women.

PROACTIVE MARKETING

Be Bold in Your Marketing

Don't market just your services or your programs.

Those are commodities. Instead, market measurable outcomes or results. Those raise the bar, set you apart and you have to deliver! E.g.: Instead of "Capsule Dressing" you would say: "*Create 10 more outfits you didn't know you had!*"

and "*Shopping in Your Closet!*" Camouflage would be: "*Discover 20 ways to look 20lbs thinner*". "Interview skills" sounds as fascinating as grass growing. Try: "*Ten Top Techniques to Win the Career of Your Dreams*".

Compare what they have now to the benefits of your services, and ask which they prefer.

Call your process or step by step system something exciting

Title it so that participants are engaged in the outcome e.g. "*Seven Steps to Fashion Freedom*", "*The Silent Secrets of Self Confidence*", "*Self-Branding: a Guide to the New Image Consciousness*".

Guarantee your results

Ask the decision-maker: "How will we know this program or consultation is a success? What outcomes or results will tell us that you got the value you want?" Find out from as many sources as possible what the problems are. Then develop your program to produce those results. You might need to involve a team and bring in your local boutiques, hairdresser and a makeup artist to help with the follow-up. Or design short, individual follow-up consultations into the price of the seminar.

Involve management in a designed follow-up

You or an attending manager could be available after the program, consultation or coaching session to check that the action plans were put in place and carried out. It costs you nothing but your time and the results are 100% more effective if participants know that they are to be held accountable.

Establish yourself as the expert

Short of writing the next definitive text on business dress, fashion trends or corporate casual, how exactly do we tell the world that we know what we are talking about and that our expertise is valuable? The trick is to get yourself into print. The written word and printed material have enormous credibility in people's minds. Yes, it would be nice to have a full-page article in USA today but just in case they haven't discovered you yet, write your own columns, booklets and articles on your favorite topics and distribute them to everyone you meet.

Write a page of frequently asked questions with your responses on interesting or pretty paper. If you have enough of those, you can compile a neat little booklet on image advice and naturally, you become the expert. Hand those out with your business card. Or for the fashion forward clients and groups, write out the top 10 fashion trends for the next season.

Send tip sheets to your local newspaper or fashion editor with your brochure. Include your tip sheet, articles and any interviews you have had when you next send out your corporate materials and brochure. You will seem more interesting and they will remember the information. At least in the follow up, you will have something to talk about.

Print the tips inside or on the back of cute, dramatic, artistic or amusing cards with your logo, name and number and hand those out to clients or at leads clubs or at networking events. You could have different cards for different topics. If you are artistic, draw your own illustrations. Distribute the cards individually or tie them up in ribbon and give out a little stack.

Linda Thomas has come out with a new book:

"My Closet, My Boutique, How to Organize Your Image". It is jam-packed with useful tips on how to boost your energy and confidence by dressing right and how to organize your closet to reduce stress. Order on-line at www.powerfulappearance.com. Fabulous!

Cecilia Stoeckicht is working with Today's Latino Magazine and wrote two articles about self esteem and the importance of image. She compared and contrasted the two cultures and suggested taking the best from each!

Marva Goldsmith has developed a workshop that gives kids in economically depressed areas:

"...a path to free yourself from the litter that clogs up the mind-works and limits your progress." The accompanying workbook "I don't need no manners 'cause I live in the hood," is distributed by Cambridge Educational Corp and Meridian Education Corp. What an inspiration!

VERBAL MARKETING

Record those tips on a cassette or video in one-minute sound bites and send them with your brochure to your local radio and TV stations. If you sound authoritative and expert-like they might include those on a talk show or magazine program. Be sure to find out the person you should send them to and follow up with a phone call. At the very least you will be on their vendor file as an expert.

Interview yourself or ask someone to interview you and write out the interview. You could do a whole series of articles with you as the expert on a variety of current image topics. Send the articles to a newspaper or give them to your clients, vendors or as handouts in workshops.

Keep referring back to events you have done and keep using testimonials from others to quote your success stories. Make sure your confident tone of voice establishes you as the expert. Leave out apologies and turn the failures into funny stories!

Use *quantifiable results* when you are promoting yourself. That way you sound like the expert and know what you are talking about. Ask your clients what happened in the interview, the date or the job as a result of their new image. Encourage them to look for *results and outcomes* in their lives. Then start quoting them.

As soon as someone in your local area or nationally becomes a news item, send a press release or an e-mail off to your newspaper, giving your opinion on their image and tips to improve it. Eventually, they will think of you as a resource. (You have to be persistent and often available on the spur of the moment.) The best way to approach the people themselves is to write a note of congratulation and include your card and a complimentary booklet or tip sheet.

WEB SITES

Design your web-site plastered with tips and topics of interest. Take a moment to look at image consultants' web sites and compare the interest level with yours. Are you selling just your services or have you included the benefits and testimonials from delighted clients and tips? If not, you may sound like everyone else in your industry. Go back and make it more interesting. Change your tips and topics regularly so people learn something new every time they visit. Very smart marketing!

PROACTIVE STRATEGIES

Make a list of all your old customers and clients. Talk to them all and find out what they are up to this year. In the course of the conversation, *find out how you can help them reach or forward their goals or New Year's resolutions.* Lock in an actual "inventing a NEW

YOU" date, even if it's several weeks ahead and send them a new marketing or "save the date' piece. Could you be the keeper of their new year's resolutions? That could turn into a longer term coaching relationship. Could you invent a new seminar and develop a follow-up coaching program for the participants' goals to succeed this year? That could expand the reach of the seminar, provide value-added services for your client and increase business for you.

Be Audacious!

Make up a new process or service or product and call it something unusual or make up a bold guarantee. Discount the service up until Valentine's Day. Then send a flyer out to clients, e-mail it or give it away to everyone you meet including all the vendors you do business with. Don't edit anyone out in your mind. Generate some energy and excitement in a world that is traditionally in the doldrums in January. Follow up and see what happens.

Reach People by Helping Their Children

What can you offer school-age children that will help them to mature or gain more survival skills? Young people are very impressionable and love anything they perceive as grown-up. Even very young children love etiquette and manners if someone other than their parents teaches them! Offer mother/daughter teas and teach them manners and etiquette. In addition, all girls dream of being models or the next Brittany Spears, so hold image and fashion classes for daughters and enlist the aid of their mothers. Then hold a class for the mothers!

Help teens and high school graduates

This segment of the population needs our services! Not only do they need interview skills but also the awareness of a realistic approach to the working world, and the skills to prepare for it. If you help people's teenagers, you will have made a friend of their parents. Join forces with local schools and institutions and put on Leadership Courses for young people.

The door reads: SNODGRASS, BULLOCK, NEVILLE, SMYTHE, & HARDWYKE, LLC.

GETTING A FOOT INSIDE THE CORPORATE DOOR

Take an extremely honest and useful look at the perception of image consultants and the industry. For the corporate world you might have to use corporate language, terms and jargon.

Position yourself as Professional Development Consultants rather than image consultants for the corporate market and provide topics that sound like professional development. Bring in image as part of a "Professional Presence" program.

Tips for Corporate Marketing

- *Be ready* to focus your training on the big picture of the organization. Start speaking bottom-line results and the effect image topics have on the culture, identity and brand of the organization.

- *Develop* certain ways to measure the effects and benefits of your training.

- *Find out* what your contact is looking for and what they need. Don't talk *at* them about your services without first asking leading questions.

- *Act* like a consultant: be versatile and work in partnership with the contact person to develop the program and even the fee structure.

- *Be prepared* to think on your feet in the sales presentation and switch your focus to match what the company is looking for.

- *Do not balk* at coming back many times. They want to get to know and trust you.

- *On the phone*, be sure to ask: "Is this a convenient time to talk?" Don't just barge into the conversation.

- *In the proposal*, include everything, even the smallest, silliest details. It is harder to go back and add when the contract has been signed.

- *When they ask* you for marketing materials, don't waste the "First Touch" on an elaborate brochure with all the bells and whistles. They simply do not have time to go through all the materials. Send an attention grabbing one-page piece that has a unique, unusual or witty appearance and shows clearly what you offer.

Get their attention when you cold call or leave a voice mail by mentioning a third party name. It will definitely help them call you back!

If you can't get the whole corporation or even one segment, ask to work with their fast-track individuals and develop a Self-Branding or Fast-Track to Promotion product. It sounds more fun, relevant and less dated than Dress for Success. Also popular is to partner with the managers of internal leadership courses to provide the skills that the company's course has not covered. These skills might include, time management, how to run an effective meeting, etiquette and business protocol, overcoming blind spots, self-promotion, presentation, body language, video critiquing, and services such as shopping for a presentation outfit, a new hairstyle and makeup.

Market to past corporate clients

But don't say: "Do you know anyone who would want (or need) my services?" Nobody can ever think of anyone when the invitation is to the whole wide world! Walter Hailey in the book: *"Breaking the No Barrier",* suggests a useful marketing process: Ask for their help. Ask what they value about you and your approach and why they bought from you. Narrow down the choices and ask them if they have any favorite **suppliers or vendors** who may have similar needs and requirements. If they suggest anyone, ask questions about this new contact and ask if your client might be willing to make an introduction. Have your own blueprint introductory letter ready that your client can pass on to the lead, (on his letterhead or e-mail), with very little work on his part to expedite the entire process, before you leave his office.

SAMPLE INTRODUCTORY LETTER

On letterhead:

From Jim Kelly

To the supplier or vendor:

Bob Jones

Dear Bob,

We have just been through an interesting branding/image/ professional presence seminar and thought of you immediately as someone who might appreciate the referral.

I would like to introduce you to the consultant who delivered the seminars on image, non-verbal communication and etiquette. The evaluations were outstanding and I can also thoroughly recommend her approach. She was funny, engaging and informative.

Her name is Jane Smith of Smith Image Consulting and not only was she extremely well received by the group, but also our people have reported since then that they have more self confidence in various situations. I think it was well worth the investment.

Her number is 123.456.7890. I also gave her your e-mail address and number and asked her to contact you.

Sincerely,
Jim

Marketing In an Economic Downturn

Just in case you have been wondering if our business is going to suffer as a result of a recession, or if you have been experiencing a few rebuttals because of the "economy", rest assured, image does play a very important part in economic downturns. You just have to know how to position it.

Pick Your Markets

Gravitate towards the people who need you most. Align with outplacement and recruitment companies. Individuals who are looking for jobs as a result of downsizing are perfect candidates for us. Point out that they will now need to differentiate their skills and talents from those of competitors with similar experience. Their visual, verbal and nonverbal presence must be consistent with the skills they are offering. "Do you look, act and sound like your resume?" is the perfect question.

Suggest to outplacement companies that you become part of a program for their high level people. They are more likely to include your services in the package they offer these people than the management layer or below. My hairstylist and I do a free seminar to the whole group at one Outplacement Company, and then get business from individuals and the company afterwards. We have even become part of the firm's advisory board.

Partner with professional development, life-style and presentation coaches. Many coaches know what is wrong with someone's appearance but do not have our training to critique and create an improved image. You can be a valuable asset to the coaching community.

Organizations are still developing their leaders, managers and fast-track employees. Image is a very important component of any in-house leadership course or individual leadership training and these people should set the example. Casual clothes might be OK in a boom economy, but as Scarlet O'Hara knew only too well when she pulled down the velvet curtains

to make a dress, you must never
look as though you are going
through rough times.

Never underestimate the power of
the beauty industry- it is almost
recession proof. Even in World War
II, clothes were scarce but women
bought lipstick and powder to boost
their morale. Show women how
they can look fantastic on a very
small budget.

Chapter 11

SELLING YOURSELF AND YOUR SERVICES

The lost art of listening

I used to talk a lot when I was selling. I thought that I needed to be fully prepared and then tell potential clients everything I had to offer. I would explain in depth all the content, the learning outcomes and the wonderful exercises in all the programs. I imagined that anything I told them from *my* point of view would be engaging and fun for *them*. And were they inspired to buy? Well, only occasionally when I found someone as fascinated in *the process* as I was. About a fraction of the population!

Now I have learned that all my clients care about is their own life. All they are asking me is: "Show me that my life is really important to YOU." So the switch in mindset for me was easy. I am

passionate about my services, but I found out that I am even more passionate about enhancing *your life*. If my services are a fit, so much the better.

Instead of spending hours preparing my proposals and working on stunning brochures, I now get all my information from my potential clients. I have found that people will buy or make changes (in their image or their corporation) if they can trust me to be the person to take them from self-protection to calculated risk. What is the secret? By getting them to *enroll* themselves into their own success by using my programs. All I have to do is to create a safe haven for them to say anything. I just listen for their infinite wisdom to emerge and hear if I can help them. This way of selling requires a skill that we all have in abundance, but rarely use to our advantage: the art of listening. When we become aware of the different ways we can listen, our conversations can become a dance between partners, not a sales call. If we can turn off the radio in our heads for a brief time, never again will we say that we are not good at selling.

Knowing that we can listen from at least three different modalities during the sales call is useful. We must be aware of the different ways we are listening, from the mind, (logical, factual, structural, and linear), the heart (passionate, emotional, sympathetic, compassionate, empathetic), or the soul, (visionary, essential, quintessential, the root of the matter, tapping into the higher being). Armed with those new distinctions, **questions, not answers** are the keys to

the kingdom. Marketing guru and Sales expert Suzanne Black, teaches our image consultant groups an infallible sales process that consists of a series of questions coming from a genuinely curious frame of mind. We all know we should listen in the sales process, but in the heat of the moment, we often find ourselves giving endless descriptions of all our services and seminars. If we let our partner do over 50% of the talking, all we need to do is to listen from the whole brain and guide the conversation to the close.

What Is Working For You?

The first thing you ask potential clients is what they are doing that they already like. (If they say, nothing, go to the second question!)

However, it is a point of entry for him to open up and talk about himself. At this point, you find out bunches of valuable information and in return validate all his good points and the way he operates. You are establishing the relationship by listening intently, from the mind.

What isn't working for you?

Listen keenly from the heart to hear their needs and issues and then from the mind for what you could provide to help them. At this point, you might need to insert a very condensed version of your services and the benefits. Ask what they think or feel about all that. Listen from the heart for excitement or caution. Answer all questions fully, map your services on their situation, and speak directly to their fears. Give appropriate case studies, funny stories, examples, and statistics that you have collected. You are now selling with humor and lightheartedness, from the heart and soul!

What is the ideal situation for you?

Now you are into the future-based part of your conversation. What would be their ideal scenario and how could your services present them with the opportunity for achieving that? Gently steer them away from the past and the issues they currently face. You are listening from the soul for their dreams, vision and what they deem important.

Allow yourself to be inspired by everything they say. That is listening from the soul!

What is stopping you?

Clients come to you with problems they cannot solve on their own or with their existing resources. Why have they not been able to solve it in the past? You are listening from the mind for what you can provide, from the soul for the essence of the issue and the common ground between you and from the heart with compassion and patience for their dilemma.

> **The Magic Questions**
> If I could help you with _____
> _____ is that something you
> would be interested in?"
> "If there were a way we could solve
> _____
> would you be interested in that?"

Once they answer these questions you know what objections you are dealing with.

Resolving your objections

More magic questions come from listening from the soul and by probing into the essence of the objection:

"Tell me more about your concerns about money/time."

"Do you have a budget in mind?"

"I heard you say you had a previous bad experience. Tell me more about that."

Listen from the heart so your responses will be sincere, but answer with a neutral statement, such as:

"I can see you might have that concern."

"I can understand."

"I can see/hear your issues." (If necessary, separate out each issue for clarification so he knows you have heard and understood them.)

Answers as questions for a close.

You are now listening from the mind for structures and solutions to fulfill his needs. Keep the conversation alive after a neutral statement with statements stated as questions such as:

"Well it sounds as if this is something you need. Would you agree"?

"Is that something you would like to do"?

"I am sensing you want to go for this...Am I right?"

"I am suggesting we do this...... Are we on track"?

"What would be our next steps?"

Closing your sale

They tell *you* what they would like to do next. Depending on the situation, a close would include requesting a deposit; sending out a questionnaire; getting a date on the calendar or in a corporate situation, sending a proposal or setting up another conversation with decision makers.

Apart from answering questions, you have not gone into vast detail about the content of your programs or services. Everything you do is now customized to their life, issue, or concern. You will find that by using all or some of this process, you and your client have created a trusting relationship that will withstand the competition and the test of time. To *listen* from those three places is an all-powerful tool.

If you mix them up and listen from the mind when they are pouring their heart out to you, you will know it immediately. The conversation will stall or take an unwelcome turn. However, you can bring it back on track, just as easily. Your client is now aware that they are special to you.

After a creative listening conversation, you are now ready to write your proposal or design your individual consultation program. You should already have the blueprint. In the case of a corporation, add their words and jargon, concerns and needs in the terms you heard them say. For an individual, include unique little features that you have heard they will appreciate.
Try this out next time you have a potential lead and see where it takes you.

Listening to your own headset is a valuable capacity to develop when speaking with your family, friends, clients, co-workers, and potential clients. You will be much less likely to have the usual "knee-jerk" reactions and what's more, you will be known as a remarkable, thoughtful person.

THE LORE AND LINGO OF THE CORPORATE MALE

Selling our services to men in corporations

"Sorry, we've hired someone else."
It was near the start of my career in the corporate world in the 80's and I was crushed. How could they possibly not want my fascinating image seminars? My first formal sales presentation, to the VP of Sales and Marketing of a large high-tech company, a bastion of an all-male corporate culture, was down the tubes.

Later, I discussed it with a male colleague. "I told the guy all about the program and went through the slides and explained everything I was going to be doing and all the benefits. What could he possibly have not liked?" I whined.

"That was your first mistake, he said. You sounded the whole time as if you were talking about individual consultations, all very complicated stuff to a guy, and you sound too touchy-feely!"

It was obvious, if I were to be successful in the corporate world, I had to learn the lore and lingo of the corporate male mentality. I hired two male consultants, one for a logo and one for content, to help me capture the attention and speak the language of a world that was largely dominated by male decision makers.

In those days, it was a revelation to me to know that men think and speak in an entirely different way than women. Not better or worse, but different, and at the very least, I needed to speak with their interests in mind. My materials needed to say that I knew about things like pro-forma, the bottom line and that I read the Wall Street Journal. (Which I did not at the time!)

Are there differences between the way men and women view the world?

From a very simplistic viewpoint, there are definitely differences! A man's psyche understands the hierarchy of a pack (think football), where competition flourishes and boundaries, orders, rules and responsibilities are well defined. He is also programmed to focus on strategies, action plans, tactics and solutions, rather than a mass of irrelevant detail. His thinking tends to be linear and logical. Women on the other hand as the so-called supportive, nurturing species are known for their collaborative efforts, co-operation, and partnership. Men have quick, solutions-oriented thinking and speaking. Women enjoy relating and talking through any issues or threatening situations to get to the result.

One interesting theory speculates that the corpus callosum, the section of the brain that connects the two hemispheres of the brain, varies. In a male brain, this section is usually thinner so men tend to use one side of their brain focusing on one problem at a time. Females on the other hand can bounce happily from one side of their brain to another, making points, expressing feelings, observations, and details to make themselves understood, build rapport, and brainstorm new ideas.

From the consultant's point of view, if we encounter a man who is not very sympathetic to "Soft Skills" training (note the terminology) it is very useful to be able to use a language that communicates more effectively and immediately to him. By the way, if you are a male reading this, the same rules apply to you!

10 Do's and Don'ts to help make the sale to very "manly" men.

1. **Do** focus on what needs to be done to fulfill his needs, not a mass of detail and confusing side issues, on topics about which he neither understands nor cares. Even if he appears fascinated about aspects of color, style, accessories and fabric, do not dwell on details in the sales presentation, just mention that they will be covered, and rest your case on the benefits.

2. **Do** ask for the problems and introduce the ways you can offer solutions. Describe an easy to understand process that you employ such as: "We do A which solves B and the benefit is C, however oversimplified that sounds to you.

3. **Do** not attempt to do the full presentation. He will be overwhelmed with all the detail and tune out. If he wants to evaluate your entire program, suggest a pilot seminar to a mixed group. You would charge a fee for this seminar.

4. **Do** not critique his outfit or correct his communication style! He has not hired you and you have not yet earned his respect. Use other examples to make your point.

5. **Do** be direct. "If only women would say what they mean. I'm not a mind-reader!" Make specific, clear requests if you want him to do something. Do not beat about the bush if you want to know if he is the decision maker or if you need to meet with his boss. Ask him!

6. **Do** make your points in linear order to form a logical conclusion. Do not jump around and bring in examples and points from all over the place. You will come across as confused, and uncertain and lacking confidence. Have an agenda or Power Point format if you are not sure of your order. He expects you to be the expert, so be it!

7. **Don't** be indecisive. "Once my wheels have been set in motion and I have decided upon a strategy, I hate to stop or change direction."

8. **Do** allow him time to mull things over. A man prefers to think about things privately and unemotionally to go through all the variables to solve the problem. Ask how long he needs to make a decision and what he would like the next steps to be.

9. "**Don't** tell me how you feel about this or that person. Do not gossip, or vent or emote or tell me that the last person has mistreated you. Tell me what you want and spare me the war stories."
VP Communications, IBM.

10. **Do** get to the point! Stick to the problem at hand and do not go off on tangents.

> *Teach these simple guidelines to your female clients. In a recent article in Business Week, the salaries of female executives were still coming in lower than their male counterparts. "Presence," or lack of it was cited as the main reason. Women lose the respect of their male colleagues by taking things too personally, being sentimental, victimized, giving excuses, and being emotional.*

NEGOTIATE YOUR WAY TO SUCCESS

- People do not buy solutions to problems they do not perceive they have.
- What do they want and how badly do they want it?
- Help people get more of what they want and less of what they do not want.

You are not likely to have to go into heavy negotiations with an individual client. You quote a set fee per hour or package of services. However, if cost appears to be a factor, (it rarely is) and if you have to play *that* game, you might negotiate a package around a few good services that can be mixed and matched. You always need to start high so the larger the package, the better the value. Then, you can always come down, not in price but in amount of services or length, or number of free extras. You might want to suggest a minimum number of services that you offer at any one session, or an hourly minimum.

Negotiating with Individuals

Too expensive /No time

"May I ask how much you are currently spending on your hair cuts, hair color, nails per year? If we were to show you how you could save three times that much on your wardrobe. Would you be interested?"

"I save my clients at least 30% of their wardrobe budget by avoiding mistakes. How many garments do you have that you do not wear regularly? What is the investment you made on those garments?"

"I shop for people in about 2 hours for clothes that last five years. How long did you spend shopping for yourself last time? How long did those clothes last?"

"My career clients gain at least 20% more in the total compensation package for the position they are interviewing for than they would have done without the new image. Would it be worth it to you to get more money for the position you want?"

"What would make this image consultation worth your time and money?"

At some point in your career, the price-hagglers need to be fired! They want the moon and the stars for next to nothing. The trick is recognizing when they become more trouble than they are worth and need to be dropped like a plate of hot cakes! The best time to fire difficult clients is just after the point you are no longer practicing, which is about three months into your career. You now have set policies and procedures, have ascertained your fees, and have taken a stand for the value you provide.

Negotiating with organizations

Organizations are used to getting the best deals. They know they wield considerable power and have a lot to offer you in terms of status and credibility. If they like you, the partnership can last for years. They value certainty and excellence. Therefore, it is often worth your while to do what it takes to earn their trust. It might take several sessions to negotiate an arrangement with a corporation that looks towards the long term. You have to decide how much you want the business. If you need their name on your client list, you will be more likely to accept their first offer. On the other hand, if you are now in the phase of your career when you can select your engagements, you will be prepared to hold out for your conditions.

Ten Commandments of Sales Negotiation:

1. Thou shalt be prepared to walk away at any stage.
2. Thou shalt listen first and speak last. He who speaketh first loseth!
3. Thou shalt be very certain of the value you offer and not give away everything upfront.
4. Thou shalt know thy bottom line and thy concessions.
5. Thou shalt not lie or manipulate but dance with thy client for a win/win.
6. Thou shalt be clear to yourself how far you will go to get the business: Know when to hold 'em and when to fold 'em.
7. Thou shalt find out what the other party is prepared to concede.
8. Thou shalt clarify progress and take action to close the deal at every stage.
9. Thou shalt copy everyone on all decisions made as people have short memories.
10. Thou shalt keep your promises and deliver more value than expected.

Find out how much they value your services

Questions to ask your client:

- "What is your ideal situation?"
- "What obstacles have you encountered?"
- "What have you done before to solve those issues?"
- "Why didn't that work?"

Create Value

The more you help other people get what they want, the more you get what you want.

Questions to ask your potential client: (As you are listening to your client, jot down the "monkeys on your shoulders" that chatter in your ears and hold you back from finding out all that is needed!)

- "What are those issues costing your company or you as an individual?"
- "Have you ever lost any business as a result of your issues?"
- "How much did that cost you or the company?"
- "If you lost reputation or good will, what do you suppose that cost you?"

> *Now you know their strengths, weaknesses, what they need, what they are prepared to pay for and why they cannot solve the problem themselves.*

Check-in steps

- ❑ "How do you feel/what do you think about what I have proposed?"
- ❑ "If I were to show you how to solve your issues (repeat their issues) would you be ready to get started?"
- ❑ "If we were able to work out the fees and payments, are you in a position to make a decision?"
- ❑ "Do you see any good reason why we should not go ahead?"
- ❑ "Would you like me to make a presentation to all the people involved in the decision?"

Find out what the objections are so you can negotiate:

Too Expensive

It is never money, always a failure to create value.

- ❑ "If I were to show you a way that you could (recreate what they say they need), would you be interested in moving forward?"
- ❑ "If we were to work out a program that suited your budget and timeframe, would you be interested?
- ❑ "If the program we have designed is too extensive/comprehensive, would you be willing to cut something out?
- ❑ "If you were willing to send more people through the program, could we talk about volume discounts?
- ❑ "If I were to show you a return on your investment, what would that be to make the program worth your while?"

In the Dance of Negotiation

"Our policy is to take only 20 per class. Everyone over that is charged 20% extra. If we could work out a way to put on more classes without charging you the extra fee, would you be interested?"
"If we were to add------------- (a concession) to the program would you be interested in working something out?
"Many companies get the per head fee from participating departments. Is that something you could consider?"
"Many companies take their budget from the end of this year and the first quarter of next. If I could work with you in quarterly payments, would that be something you could consider?"

The Aztecs were wise people.

Their four components for a relationship to be successful were:

Trust 52%

Respect 26%

Acceptance 13%

Admiration 9%

Where else can you use these negotiation skills?

- Buying from vendors
- Negotiating with a hotel for conference space
- Bartering with strategic alliance partners, ex-husbands, children etc.

Chapter 12

HOW TO BEAT THE COMPETITION WITH A WINNING PROPOSAL

You have been asked to write a proposal that could translate into a large proportion of your yearly revenues, if you play your cards right and think big. How do you approach this task when you do not know much about the situation, but you do know that the company is going to ask other consultants? This is called a Bid, or Request for Proposal (RFP).

How do you handle an RFP?

Ask yourself...

- ❑ Have I heard their needs and can I repeat them in their language?
- ❑ Can I translate those into a program or programs appropriate to their group?
- ❑ What are the benefits of my program to participants and the company?
- ❑ How am I qualified to facilitate the program?
- ❑ Have I done this (or at least pieces of this) successfully before?
- ❑ How am I going to organize the program, logistics, people, and time involved?
- ❑ What fee structure am I charging?

Here are some do's and don'ts to start off		
Do this	**Say this**	**Result or Option**
Write down every single thing you want in the proposal, so you can negotiate when the time comes.	Our trainers require at least three-star level hotels for overnight stays.	You can always use this as a point of negotiation.
Do you charge for travel time?		Many consultants charge a lower rate and put it in the proposal.
Make the proposal detailed so the client can feel, touch, and visualize your program. You want to make it real for them.	*For our top-level program:* "We bring in hair and makeup experts and partner with a clothing store, or "We provide a 40-page workbook that follows the seminar outline."	If you have to negotiate, ask them: "If I bring down my fee, what would you like me to cut out of the program?"
Write down verbatim every need you hear them say. People want to know that you have listened, heard, and understood their problems.	You may have to say the same thing in many different ways.	
Write the benefits of your consulting and courses separately from the course topics and the objectives.		Sell the sizzle *and* the steak.
Write the benefits for all the parties concerned.	Company, participants and managers, or supervisors.	

Here are some do's and don'ts to start off		
Do this	**Say this**	**Result or Option**
Don't be generic.	If you say, "Participants gain awareness of image concepts."	Great line, but what exactly do they learn?
Do not try to be all things to all people or you will lose credibility. Demonstrate that you are the expert in your field.	We recommend that people from the same financial level be in the same group.	E.g. entry-level personnel, managers, and executives.
Add value-added touches here and there that show you are worth your fee.	Follow-up phone calls and coaching are included.	If you are pushed to negotiate, these are areas you can leave out if you need to drop your price. (You could drop these off the program or include them in your fee if they were the deal breaker.)
Have a section titled: Our Recommendations.	For best results we recommend individual 20 minute follow-up sessions.	You position yourself as the experts with experience.
Write a very clear expense or investment page for your client and his managers.	Include two or three options but not more. People love to be presented with a few good choices. They will flip to this page first so make sure the bottom line is crystal clear.	Complicated accounting and unclear fee structures may discount you.
Make the presentation of your document exquisite, creative, and professional.	Make sure every section is clear in larger typeface than normal and graphically pleasing.	You are in the image business and so are your materials Use white space creatively.

Here is an outline for a proposal:

A. **The Situation**

For a large proposal, you need to describe the general issues of the situation at hand or the industry-wide problems that your client can identify. This short paragraph shows that you understand their problem, sets the stage, justifies your existence, and puts the issues to be addressed in a context.

B. **The Needs**

Position yourself as part of the needs:

E.g. *ABC Company seeks a top consultant, or (a team of top consultants) familiar with corporate branding, image, appearance, hair, makeup and nonverbal communication to provide consulting and seminars to the groups involved.*

In this section, you would set out in bulleted format exactly what you have heard your client says he needs. Use his words, phrases, and industry terminology. Sometimes a "want" has to be translated into a need to which your program can supply the answer. For example, a hotel manager might want all his front desk personnel to have the same look. His needs are:

- Development or review of the uniform;

- Makeup, grooming and hair workshop

- Image training to achieve consistency with the hotel brand.

C. **The Program**

Write out one program in detail with learning objectives or, if there are multiple programs, write out the topics covered under each segment. Develop the time-line for the various groups who would take the classes and how you would space the program series. Remember although *you* are fascinated with your process and program, your client does not need to know how you will conduct it. At this stage, he just needs to know some learning objectives and a synopsis of the material. The details can be fleshed out when you have the assignment.

D. The Benefits

More important at the proposal stage are the benefits of your program.

If your benefits contain some specific measurements and results that you can personally guarantee, so much the better. If you are not sure about the long-term benefits, state the benefits of the program itself.

A very good tip here is to separate the benefits for each group involved and have about three or four benefits for each. For example:

- **The company:** Enhancement of the corporate identity in the marketplace.

- **The participants:** Participants learn valuable tips and techniques to organize their closet and save time and money on their working wardrobe.

- **The managers or supervisors:** The sales department will have the communication skills necessary to resolve internal conflicts and reduce external complaints by an average of 70%.

E. Our Recommendations

Here you would take charge of the situation. Outline exactly what you want in terms of class size, group type and homogeneity, pre-course meetings, post course debriefing, measurements and other proofs of the success of the program, the design of the uniforms, other experts you would like to bring in to help you with hair, makeup, and clothes. If you have this well thought out, you will sound much more like an experienced consultant who is going to partner with the company to help it achieve its goals.

F. **The Investment**

Make an outline of the fees, the cost of a possible pilot, and the cost of a volume discount. You should also list a synopsis of what the fee includes; just in case this page is separated from the proposal and a new set of people receive only this page.

This section would also include any proposed, exact, or approximate expenses. The expensed items should be clearly delineated between those that will be included in your fee such as handouts, and the expenses such as workbooks, hotel, room, meals, and transportation that will be billed to the company.

G. **Your Qualifications**

Your biography should be written with details relevant to the situation. For example, if this were a proposal for a university group, you would be wise to mention your degrees and educational background. A business organization on the other hand might be more interested in your previous business experience, even if it is not image related. Always include results as well as descriptions in your bio. E.g., state what happened as a result of your work in a certain company or project, not just your work description or title.

H. **References**

Your potential client always wants to know if you have had any experience in his industry. If you have not, give him references from your clients who have had similar issues. Then coach your reference clients on what to say and how to say it! If you do not make these preliminary preparations, you risk that the testimonial they give will be too generic and vague. That might translate to your potential client that you did not do a great job!

SAMPLE CONTRACT

Ms. Susan Smith

ABC Company

1000 Main Street

City, State, Zip.

Date:

Contract between _____and Your Name Image Company

Your Name Image Company agrees to enter into this contract with _____for

one full-day seminar at the _____ Hotel, your town.

Scheduled Date:

Fees:

Full day:

Expenses, travel, board, lodging, and materials paid by the client. All workbooks to be

ordered in advance of the seminar are non-refundable.

CANCELLATION FEE:

If the seminar is canceled by Your Name Image Company due to an emergency, Your

Name, (President) will promise to reschedule the seminar within 30 days of the original

date.

If the seminar is cancelled within 30 days prior to the seminar date by (Your client's

name) _____payment is to be made in full to Your Name Image

Company.

Fifty percent of the payment is requested one week prior to the seminar date and the

balance on the day of the seminar (Or whatever payment schedule you have worked out).

Please sign and fax this contract back to

(Your Name) at: ---. ---. ----

Signed_____

Date_____

Signed_____

Date_____

Chapter 13

WORKING WITH THE MEDIA

The media is in business to make money and report on the latest controversy or issue! If you contact the media, or are contacted by them, you will need to come across as professional with ideas that are current and targeted towards the audience or reader. A small local publication might report that you have launched your business, especially if you are the first to offer this type of service in your town, but generally, large circulation magazines or newspapers will need a newsworthy pitch, angle, or story from which to write a larger article. You will also need to respond very quickly to a phone call or email, because the media world is fast paced and deadline oriented. They may have contacted several image consultants to get views immediately on this or that topic.

If you appear on TV, make sure that your hair, makeup, and outfit are appropriate for the target audience and the segment you are representing. The majority of the audience needs to identify with you and with your message. Don't appear too hip, trendy, alluring, or so classic that you look dated.

APPEARANCE GUIDELINES FOR TV

Dress

- Bring two outfits just in case.
- Structured clothing works best to give your body a good shape. A tailored, set in shoulder or soft shoulder padding will be most flattering.
- Show off your neck, top of your chest, ear lobes and jaw line and choose a neckline that frames your jaw line.
- Avoid sparkling, metallic, transparent, very stiff, or wrinkled fabrics.
- Avoid huge earrings, buttons, and necklaces. Keep accessories small to medium with no shine.

The fit should be impeccable. Check that the garment does not pull or strain anywhere.

- Avoid thick, wooly, and napped fabrics and unconstructed styles. They add weight and TV already adds 5-10lbs.
- Stick to solids in pastels or medium to deep shades.
- Avoid plaids, polka dots, checks, topstitching, contrasting piping, horizontal lines, color blocking, patch pockets, epaulets, and gathers around the waist. They all add pounds.
- Avoid animal, floral, and large scale wildly colored prints.
- Keep colors in the light to medium range and the warmer tones actually retain their color better than cool colors.
- Ivory and cream are better than ice white. Avoid black.
- Avoid scarves, which slip and slide around.
- Wear a jacket with a lapel to hold the microphone clip, and choose separates (instead of a dress) for easier concealment of the wires!

Makeup

Every little imperfection is picked up by the camera. So make sure your skin is in good condition. Drink water, use moisturizers, and get lots of sleep before your appearance. Alcohol and cigarettes will dry out your skin do don't calm your nerves with a drink or smoke! The makeup for TV is rather thick and will need to be in a deeper shade than your own skin color. Normal makeup will not cover your skin adequately or take the lighting well, so a camouflage makeup might be appropriate. Although you will go heavier on your skin coverage, the rest of your makeup will seem lighter than normal. Blending is Critical.

- Use a VERY light warm toned blush for eye shadows
- Use a VERY light blush to add minimal color to the apple of the cheekbone. Any color will be exaggerated by TV.
- Avoid frosted and dark eye shadows. They look dated.
- Use a soft brown or black eye shadow for eyeliner.

- Mascara the top lashes only, unless you have very blonde lashes.
- Tweeze and shape your eyebrows as they add a frame to the face.
- Define your lips with a pencil the same color as the lipstick and avoid a matte shade of lip color with little to no sheen or gloss.
- Powder everything and bring extra powder with you.

Hair

Think of TV and photographs as two-dimensional. Both the external and internal (around your face) silhouettes of the hairstyle are very important, so take a good look at the shape of your face and choose a hairstyle that does not repeat the shape of your face. The oval is the most pleasing shape, and your hairstyle can be used to shorten, lengthen, slim down, or widen a face shape. Very dark hair can provide a stark contrast and diminish your facial features. Consider warmer low lights around your face for the camera, and grow your very short style hair for your appearance, as very short hair tends to disappear on the camera.

- Choose a slightly longer style which allows for movement and volume.
- Avoid hair that covers half your face, which can be distracting for the viewers, especially if you have to keep flipping it back.
- Side parts are more flattering than central parts.
- Avoid a style that is tightly drawn back from your face. Use the hair as a soft frame.
- Choose a low maintenance hairstyle that is easy to style and you can forget when you are on camera.

Make It Meaningful

Always link image to some trend or newsworthy topic. Nothing generic. Keep the sentences short, and tell the story in 40 seconds.

1. Send timely, trendy ideas to the associate editor of a newspaper, the program director in radio and the News director in TV.
2. Suggest five stories, angles, or pitches that could be made out of one topic. Be very focused.

3. Don't give up. Material is passed from department to department and may be used by someone other than your initial contact.

4. Know what the formula of the TV/radio program is, e.g., heavy or light news.

5. Don't send a video to the radio station!

6. Find out how they would like to be contacted; no lunches, breakfasts or coffee breaks, unless they want to interview you in person. It is best to use phone, video, or audio tape or e-mail the press release or idea.

7. Attention -grabbing packaging works.

8. Call them back, don't take no personally.

9. Drop names, it helps them call you back.

10. Provide your interviewer with 10 questions to ask you and include some unusual ones that they would not have thought of.

11. Interview like a politician! If you are being interviewed on one topic and have a message, you really want to get across, answer all the questions you are asked and be subtle about weaving in your message.

Hot topics for the Media:

- How to adapt fashion to look hot for Spring/ Autumn.
- Three common foot problems and how to solve them.
- Baby yoga!
- Natural cold and flu remedies and how to look good with a cold.
- How to look taller, richer, thinner, younger sexier!
- How to orchestrate a successful first impression.
- **Tips:** How to remove stains; how to avoid dry cleaning.
- How to deal with rudeness in the workplace
- How to add humor in the workplace to overcome stress.
- How to save three solid weeks of time in your year by knowing how to shop.
- How to save $23,000 in a lifetime by knowing the right clothes to buy.

Use statistics and studies that prove how useful we are to people's budgets, time management and image management strategies. The information from the study below for example, could spawn many articles and interviews from our sector!

A 2006 UK study of 2000 British women, by Churchill Home Insurance found that women spend 7 billion GBP buying clothes, shoes, and accessories they will never wear, that languish in the closet. In fact, on average, they had 305 GBP (about $550) in one year and 12,810 GBP ($23,000) worth of clothes in a lifetime. That's a down payment on something big! Men had on average nine items of clothing they never wore, mostly shirts! If this is the case, don't you think that pretty much everyone could use a bit of advice from us?

How to Write a Press Release

Follow a few simple steps and you can get your name and news in your local newspaper. If you get your name on their list of experts, you will be called time and time again!

The main thing to remember in a press release is that features or fashion writers want you to make their job easy; so write the release in a format that they can transpose and use directly. Journalists are trained to put all the important details into the first few paragraphs because they know that editors cut from the bottom of the article. The media is hungry for breaking news but it all has to have a different spin and a current slant. Your message needs to be relevant to the medium you are pitching to: newspapers, television, radio, or magazines. Keep the language simple and the content interesting. Capture them with a strong lead or headline.

The following example is fictitious but the format should follow these general guidelines:

- Name of participating company
- Your name as the contact person
- Your number
- Your e-mail address
- Today's date

Headline To Grab The Attention:

Career Tips for Jobless help Graduating Minorities Beat the Odds.

WHO: Image Consultant Susan Jones, President of Career Enhancement Inc. works with minority graduating students of Lark Forest Community College.

WHAT: A unique, accelerated process including career tips and real-life interview practice with employers, image, verbal communication and body language helps graduating students get the edge in interviews.

WHERE: Seminars now available to minorities outside the college every month at the College Community Center. Fee: $125

WHEN: First Saturday of every month. 9:00 am to 6:00 pm.

WHY: At the current 6%, unemployment is at an all time high. This program has been proven to help minority students strengthen their resumes, enhance their interview skills and ultimately get jobs quicker than average in this economic down-market.

A press release could also be in the form of a mini article. If the newspaper sub-editor is interested, he will call you and write his own version with your quotes or use most of what you have written and embellish it, as in this example:

Contact: Susan Jones

231-347-4545

July 25, 2003

Career Seminar Helps Graduating Minorities Beat the Odds

Miami, FL- Susan Jones, an image consultant and professional development specialist has established a unique approach to interviews for minority graduate students of Lark Forest Community College graduating classes.

The first Saturday of every month, Susan, a 10-year veteran in image, teaches a seminar that provides the students with real-life experiences they would never get in the normal classroom situation. The day starts with interview skills, image critiques and resume instruction.

"At the current 6%, unemployment is at an all time high," said Jones. "This program has been proven to help minority students strengthen their resumes, enhance their interview skills and ultimately get jobs quicker than average in this economic down-market."

The class lasts from 9 am to 6 pm, and is now open to minorities outside the college. Towards the end of the seminar, real employers and Human Resource professionals are invited in to give the students interview questions and provide feedback on their answers.

"This approach has accelerated the students' learning curve," said Susan Jones, President of Career Enhancement Inc. "As a result, many of these students who find English a challenge, are gaining more confidence and getting jobs in record time."

Anyone interested in taking the course should contact Susan Jones by August 4.

Radio Interviews

Radio stations do not deal with information in the same way as magazines or newspapers. Radio is paid for one thing only: an abundance of new listeners; and it will flourish on anything that attracts them. Since the nature of radio news and features is through verbal communication, the most engaging way to disseminate information via radio is through controversial interviews. If you approach a radio station with a story, you will need to shape it so that it sounds controversial and attracts as wide an audience as possible. Radio hosts love guests to quote facts, tidbits, and statistics gleaned from feature stories and news.

Start with "Did you know that …" and present some shocking facts that substantiate your point and knock down some sacred cows or pre-conceived notions.

Become a master at presenting any image topic, not straight but with a twist.
To turn straight information into a controversial topic, think about the way people argue both sides of a case. Then take one side, do your research, if possible include statistics and case studies or stories and offer your topics to the radio stations.
Here are some examples:

Boring Topic	Pique interest	Controversial
Weight loss	Pit one diet against another like a football game. Facts about Weight Watchers versus South Beach. Calories vs. high carbohydrate.	Are all diets dangerous? Come up with startling facts about the health risks.
Men's skin care	How men can attract women with new beauty products for men. The sexual attraction of scents and their meaning.	Gay and straight skin care products, is there a difference? Are metro sexual (straight, fashion-conscious) men catching up with the gay skin-care market?
Career and Interview Techniques	The top twenty mistakes people make in interviews.	What Headhunters won't tell about getting the interview.
	Secrets from an expert to increase your compensation package.	Can image increase your odds of getting the job by 20%?
	How to beat out the competition with "body politics".	Can interviewers tell if you are lying - Is your body language leaking?

Chapter 14

GETTING A BOOK PUBLISHED

By Jill Bremer, AICI, CIP

Bremer Communications

www.bremercommunications.com

One of the fastest ways to create a buzz and build credibility in the image business (or any business for that matter) is to write a book and have it published. In 2004, my first book was published by Financial Times Prentice Hall. Written with co-author and friend, Cyndi Maxey, It's Your Move: Dealing Yourself the Best Cards in Life and Work, was the fulfillment of a life-long dream for me. It was one of the most difficult things I've ever done, but also one of the most rewarding. This book brought us renewed credibility, lots of visibility and media attention, and an additional revenue stream for our businesses.

I believe we all have book inside us just waiting to be written. Don't be scared and don't tell yourself you can't do it. Believe me, if we could do it, anyone can do it! We didn't know anything about the publishing business when we started, but we learned along the way. What follows is an account of what we learned. May it provide you with the insight and strategies that will propel you and your expertise into the bookstores and the hands of the buying public.

Getting Started

In the summer of 2001, I received a phone call from my good friend. Already a published author herself, she asked me to consider co-authoring a new book. I knew having a book published would be a smart move for my career and business. I already had a successful Internet newsletter, had a few articles published in trade journals, and was in the middle of guest authoring a chapter for another person's book. So I jumped at the chance. She recently had a co-authored book published and knew she liked having a writing partner. She explained that having a co-author made the process more fun, we'd be able to keep each other on task, and we'd be able to split many of the other jobs related to writing a book.

Of course, if you want to write a book by yourself – and are a <u>very disciplined</u> person – go for it!

With whom could you partner to write a book? Who has expertise that complements yours?

As we started talking, we didn't have a clue as to what our topic should be. She asked me to brainstorm about what I have a passion for; those topics that I love most to write about, talk about, or teach others.

What do you most love to write about, talk about, or teach others?

She and I both shared our ideas. Cyndi then took our combined list and conducted research to find the current trends to which we could tie our expertise. Trends and current events are what the media write about and you, of course, need media attention in order to sell your books! For instance, can you relate what you know to the American "baby boomers," unemployment, the increase in incivility, or changes in technology? Do you have an unusual slant on your topics that no one else has?

You want whatever you write to be both topical and timely. This is what will get you into the newspapers, on radio and TV. Remember – there are no new ideas, only new ways to package them.

What is your unique slant on your topics? To what current events or trends can you tie your expertise?

The current event we wanted to tie to was the unemployment crisis taking place at that time in America and we felt we had a lot of helpful image and communication information to share with readers. We scheduled weekly phone calls to pull together our ideas and book proposal. We took time at this point to discuss our joint goals for this project and agreed that we wanted the following: to be published by a well-known New York publishing company, to get a book placed into major bookstores, and to write a book that could drive our business.

What are you goals for writing a book?

We also searched bookstores and their web sites for other books that sounded similar to our themes. We knew publishers and the buying public would see these books as our competition and we wanted to be familiar with their slants on the topics. We also searched these web sites for books that might pop up with our proposed book titles and for the names of the publishing companies who published similar books. We thought if they were interested in one book on the topic, they might be interested in another.

What could be a clever title for your book?

Book Proposals

Now that we had an idea of what we wanted to write about, we set out to write a book proposal, one that would catch the eye of literary agents. We didn't know anything about proposals or agents, so once again we went to the Internet to conduct our research. We found The Literary Marketplace, www.literarymarketplace.com, to be an excellent resource. It lists literary agents and publishers around the world. Click on the names and you'll find contact information, and often web links, to

hundreds of agents. Most agents' web sites will offer directions for book proposal submissions. Research several of them and you'll have a good grasp of what a book proposal should include. Based upon what we learned online, we created a master book proposal with a number of elements so that, no matter what an agent requested, we had the material ready to create a customized mailing.

Our master proposal included:

<u>Overview</u>

- CONCEPT AND PURPOSE
  Explain what this book will offer to readers. Ours included phrases such as:
  "A practical guide for…"
  "Offering strategies…"
  "This book is designed to…"
- SPECIAL FEATURES
  Describe the unique features your book will include, such as interviews, quizzes, etc.
- AUTHOR OVERVIEW
  Biographies

Market

- AUDIENCE

  Describe the types of readers or demographics your book will target.

- COMPETITION

  Compare and contrast similar books, noting how none are quite like yours.

- THE PACKAGE

  Explain the visual look of your book: hard or soft cover, dimensions, number of pages, illustrations, etc.

About The Authors

- WHAT WE SHARE

  As co-authors, we detailed how our expertise complements the other.

- LONGER BIOS

  Longer-length bios that include personal as well as professional information.

- PROMOTABILITY

  Promote your ability to sell your book. Talk about your demand as a speaker, your marketing savvy, etc.

Outline

- TABLE OF CONTENTS

  List the chapters with a short description of what each will cover

Additional Enclosures:

- Two sample chapters
- Other writing samples (published articles, etc.)

Working with an Agent

Once your proposal is written, it's time to start shopping it around to literary agents. Why get an agent? They're "plugged in" to the publishing world and already have established relationships with publishers. In fact, many publishers will only look at proposals that were sent to them by agents. Agents will be your representative in the negotiation process and will help you get the best deal and advance money. In addition, their job is to secure a deal not only for publishing, but also for TV, film, video, audio, and merchandising. Agents are also very helpful providing feedback and guidance.

Along with the names of agents you gathered from The Literary Marketplace, you can also find names by reading the Foreword section of books already published, where many authors name and thank their agents. Also, make a list of everyone you know personally who might possibly know an agent. Start working your network; talk to other authors, neighbors, colleagues, high school friends, etc.

Whom do you know who might know a literary agent?

Some agents may ask for materials to be sent electronically, others will want hard copies of everything to be sent via mail. Be sure to package your proposal in a nice folder and include a cover letter. Send out only 5-10 proposals at a time; it's easier to track responses and is less expensive. You may get an agent with the first small batch you send out. We actually found our agent through a connection Cyndi's husband made at his high school reunion, someone who does marketing in the publishing field who offered to hand-deliver our proposal to an agent friend of his! That person loved our proposal and quickly became our

agent. We liked him right away because he was experienced, well connected in publishing, and was excited about our book idea. Very important - you want to work with an agent who truly loves your book.

Agents will shop your proposal to the publishing houses and will keep you posted as to the feedback they receive. He or she will also be able to advise you if a change in focus is needed in your proposal. After a few rejections, our agent asked us to change our book direction from "business" to "self-help." At that time, business books were hard to sell; self-help books were more appealing to publishers and can also reach a much larger audience. So we reworked our proposal, our agent sent it out, and the first publisher who saw it expressed interest. A few days later, our agent had lunch with this editor (a good argument for having an agent based in the same city as the publishers). He was able to glean a lot of helpful information during that lunch and prepared us for the big phone call to come.

CONTRACTING WITH THE PUBLISHER

During our first phone call with the editor, he was very interested in two things: the size of our audiences at our speaking engagements and who our book endorsers might be. This seemed to be as important as our book's content – did we have what it would take to sell it?

How many people could you speak to during the first year of your book's release?

Whom do you know who might be willing to endorse your book?

We ended that phone call with a verbal assurance that he wanted to publish our book. It was many weeks before we had the actual contract in our hands, but we moved forward writing the book. He had given us a deadline about 6 months away, and we knew we couldn't waste any time.

When the contract arrived, it was four pages long plus addendums, and written in very tiny print. We tried to understand it, but it was too difficult. We decided to hire a lawyer who specializes in working with authors and publishing contracts. I strongly recommend that you do the same, and to do so, you will need to budget accordingly. Lawyers can be expensive upfront, but can save you money and many headaches in the long run. We were able to negotiate a contract that:

- Allowed us to own the copyright to our material (which enables us to use our content in other formats – web sites, workbooks, etc.)
- Gave us the right to do derivative works based upon our content (such as seminar workbooks, articles, etc.)
- Stipulated that the publisher must publish our book within 18 months (to make sure we were published promptly)
- Stipulated that, if they ever stop printing our book, the rights to publish the book will be turned over to us (so that we can self-publish this book later, if we choose to do so.)

We felt these elements were what any consultant or speaker would want and we were pleased when the publisher agreed to our list of requests.

WORKING WITH THE PUBLISHING COMPANY

When you work with a publishing company, you will have many people assigned to help you with your project. Before we had even signed the contract, a development editor notified us that he would be working with us. His job was to shape our writing so that it would be clear and as marketable as possible. We emailed him the chapters as they were finished; he marked them up with suggested changes and sent them back to us to rework. We also had a tech reviewer looking at our drafts. She helped us with our quoted material and grammar. We did all of this collaboration via email and phone. In fact, we never met face-to-face with any of the people who worked with us on our book.

Our team included:

- Executive Editor – the person who read our proposal and signed us to a contract
- Two Development editors – see above
- Layout company – handled the layout of the inside book content
- Art Director – oversaw the graphic elements of our book
- Cover designer – did the design of the front and back book covers
- Index editor – created the book index
- Sales Team – handled the corporate sales of our book, also helped us set up our web sites to sell books ourselves
- Publicists – consisted of a small sales team internally; we also hired our own publicity team

We learned early on that all of these people had different communication styles and preferences for communication – email, phone, etc. Learn your teams' preferences as soon as possible. Also, find out who is employed part-time vs. full-time, in-house employee vs. outside contractor, time zones where they're located, and names of assistants who work for them. All of this information will help you "hit the ground running" and be productive and effective from the moment you start.

Publicity – Your Efforts And Theirs

You can't sell books without publicity - and you can't do publicity all by yourself. You'll need a strategy, you'll need to know how to write a good press release, and you'll need to know who to reach within the media. When we got to this point in the process, we quickly realized that the writing of the book was a small piece of the total puzzle. We found publicizing the book takes as much effort – and probably more time - than the actual writing of the book itself. Other authors had advised us that, in the current economic climate, big publishers weren't investing much into a book's publicity; it was up to the authors to supplement the publisher's efforts, (which is why they want to know upfront the size of your speaking audiences)! What we didn't know was how much a professional publicity campaign can cost, which is tens of

thousands of dollars. We knew that if we were going to do any publicity on our own, it would have to be on a shoestring. Our publisher assigned us a publicist (an independent contractor) who was given a 2½-month lead-time to build interest before the book was released. She developed the publisher's "official" press release announcing the impending release of the book, which was sent out to various media people. That press release generated coverage in a number of magazines, newspapers, and executive newsletters, including a review by a syndicated columnist that was picked up in many papers throughout the country. Our contract with the publisher stipulated that we would each receive 25 free copies of the book. When we talked more with the publisher about how speakers and trainers can generate more speaking engagements by sending out books as calling cards, they asked for mailing lists from both of us and sent several hundred books to our clients and prospects. Don't be afraid of asking for hundreds of books. At first, it will look to them as lost sales, but you can easily position it as potential for increased sales.

In addition to the first publicist, we decided to hire our own public relations strategist. This person taught us about reaching the media; she devised a game plan for our efforts, and also created for us customized media lists. She was herself a book publicist, but also made her expertise available as a strategist. She was very helpful and the media lists she built for us were invaluable. Now, we just had to do all the work! We decided to find an intern to help us. We posted a free ad on the web site for the Public Relations Student Society of America (www.prssa.org), as one author-friend suggested we do. The first person that responded had a major in Journalism and Public Relations minor. She also lived in our area. We interviewed her and hired her immediately – and it was one of the best things we ever did. We worked quite well as a team. Cyndi and I wrote the press releases, our intern shaped them up and sent them out to our media contacts. She also handled all of the follow-up, sending books out as requested, and

always kept the two of us informed. She also took the initiative to research additional media contacts for us. Interns generally work for free (you pay for expenses, of course), although some "thank you" money from time to time is a nice - and appreciated - gesture.

Our strategist urged us to create press releases that were tied to current themes in the news. For instance, we wrote releases about the "jobless recovery" and the "rebounding job market" and teased how our book had helpful solutions. We also wrote many releases that related our book to various days named in Chases' Calendar of Events, a wonderful resource book you can find at public libraries and online. Chase's lists thousands of themed days, weeks, and months, such as Common Courtesy Day (March 17th), Better Conversation Week (November 22-28), and Image Improvement Month (January). These releases brought us much attention from the media and our releases, as well as the interviews they produced, were in papers around the country.

SAMPLE PRESS RELEASE

For Immediate Release

Contact: *Jill Bremer*   ***Cyndi Maxey***

(708) 848-5945 (W)   (773) 561-6252 (W)

(708) 848-6254 (H)   (773) 275-5285 (H)

Jill@Bremercommunications.com   cmaxey@cyndimaxey.com

December 30th is No Interruptions Day!

Authors' New Book Can Help You Make the Most of this Day!

Chicago, IL—December 1, 2003- If you have ever had a full eight hours of in-office time to devote strictly to getting work done, you know what *really* happens: About one-third of those hours are spent in actual, productive phone calling, research, writing and emailing. The rest are spent answering non-priority calls, getting sidetracked by email or conversations you did not expect, and generally getting distracted by the minutiae of life and work!

In their new book, **It's Your Move: Dealing Yourself the Best Cards in Life and Work**, (Financial Times Prentice Hall, ISBN: 0-13-142481-5, $22.95, October 2003) authors Cyndi Maxey and Jill Bremer discuss ways to play your cards right so that you achieve the goals you set for yourself. If you want to work better against all the interruptions you encounter, here are some of their tips:

1. Plan ahead. Write down the three main things that you want to get done today.
2. Make a list of all the steps needed to achieve those three major tasks. That way, if you do get interrupted, you will be able to get back on track quickly.
3. Turn off everything electronic that you do not need to achieve those goals. This could mean silencing your phone, computer, or CD player.
4. Turn off your email program if it does not accomplish one of your three goals.
5. Get caller ID on your business line. It is well worth it!
6. Post a sign on your door or wall. The sign should say, "Please do not bother me—I'm concentrating!"
7. If someone insists on interrupting you, listen to what they have to say (without interrupting!) and then tell him or her clearly and concisely that you understand what they said, but that you are busy with another project at the moment. Finish by telling them what you *are* willing to do for them and when it could be done.

8.   Keep a water bottle nearby to avoid leaving the desk for drinks.

These are just a few of the many useful tips Maxey and Bremer provide in It's Your Move. Their book provides numerous inspiring personal examples and winning strategies for the games we play in life and career.

Amy Lindgren, columnist for the Twin Cities Pioneer Press, writes: "Maxey and Bremer are two of the most optimistic, yet practical, authors I've had the pleasure to read in the field of career development. From the first paragraph of the introduction, they had me hooked." Best-selling author Bob Nelson, Ph.D., notes that "Cyndi Maxey and Jill Bremer have crafted a tutorial for life through with anybody could benefit. Both reflective and practical, it serves as the best friend you always wanted that forced you to look in the mirror when you most needed to see the truth."

By concentrating on the tasks at hand with the help of these useful tips, you can plan a successful and fruitful No Interruptions Day!

# # #

If you'd like to mount a professional publicity campaign, my advice is to start saving money now. We heard of one author who started saving money for his publicity one year before he even started writing the book. At the time we wrote our book, publicists' fees ranged from $5,000.00 to $8,000 per month with a 3-6 month minimum. Radio tours (30 phone interviews with talk radio stations) were priced at $3,300.00. Some authors we've talked to set aside their entire advance money as their publicity fund.

Besides sending out press releases to the media, there are some other things you can do to build awareness of your book.

- Use email and send information about your book to all of your clients and prospects. Send them book synopses, a few of the press releases you write, web links to your reviews in print, etc. Getting a book into their hands is a great idea, but keeping them "in the loop" in other ways can build their interest and their ability to pass the word along to others.
- Develop a one-hour mini-workshop on your book that you can market to clients and prospects. It's a great way to give new and current audiences a teaser of your book's content and sell some books at the same time.

- Have postcards designed and send them out as a direct mail campaign. We had four-color postcards created announcing the book release that included our photos, cover art, testimonials, ordering instructions, and intro workshop details. We bought several mailing lists from groups we had targeted as good prospects and sent out hundreds of cards.

- Apply to speak at national conferences. Associations are often interested in featuring speakers who are newly published. You'll reach large audiences and will be able to sell your book onsite after your workshop and in the conference bookstore. Keep in mind that associations call for proposals many months in advance of their conference dates. We sent proposals to a few associations before we even finished writing the book!

Your book will only be considered new for one year after it's released. So, strike while it's hot. Create a publicity strategy – and budget – at the same time you begin the writing process. Your publicity efforts may take more time and effort than writing the book itself, but it will pay off in the long run with increased sales and public attention.

So, what should you do now? Put on your thinking caps, fire up the computer, and just start writing. Don't let another day go by dreaming about the book you've always wanted to write. Just do it – you'll be so glad you did!

Publishing Your Own Book

Print on Demand Publishers

If you don't have the time to scout around for your own agent or have drawn a blank in finding a boutique publisher who will take your book, don't lose heart. If you have a sneaking suspicion that your book will be well received by a niche market or even the general public; there are a few other avenues available to you.

Traditionally, when large and small publishers alike accept a book from an author there is quite a risk involved. For that reason the publishing industry, like bankers, want to protect their investment. Consider for a moment the publishing process. Before a single book has been sold, publishers might have to pay the author an advance, or sum of money; they also have to print books in vast quantities. The publisher may have to store the books in warehouses for years until the first edition sold out.

Since the inventory is so high and the layers of publishing, warehousing and distribution so complex, the book business was and is a risky business. If the book did not sell, the author had to cart them home and fill his attic and basement with 40 tons of books.

In recent years, many of the small publishing houses were not able to make a profit and merged with large multinational publishing houses. Naturally, these were in business to make large profits and only dealt with books presented by a book agent, or ones they considered would be an excellent bet, or written by established authors. The niche book market was in danger of dying out and young authors had no way of becoming established. These first-time or young authors had two ways to publish: Self-publishing was one (the author does everything); vanity press was another (the author pays a publisher to get everything done and still has to print a minimum run of books).

Luckily, in the past ten years two new technologies have revolutionized the printing industry: First, a process to print one book cost effectively; and second, the internet. Small runs of books became easy to print and web sites became the distribution channel of choice for many authors. Voila'! The Print on Demand, POD industry started to flourish. Print on Demand is a strategic alliance between the author and the publisher to get one book at a time printed and sent to the buyer, some bookstores, some on-line bookstores, or the library.

There are pros and cons to POD but if you can market your book directly to your clients, from your web site and at your seminars and workshops, you might consider this as the first option when contemplating writing a book. Just in case you think you might start with a POD book and then get "discovered," rest assured, it is highly unlikely. As it stands right now, the two relationships are distant cousins and traditional publishing houses consider any POD book to be, by definition, not worth bothering about.

However, the pros for POD are considerable. The royalties for POD are greater than for publishing; there is no

agent provocateur to interfere in the relationship with the publisher, and you as the author have no boxes of books piled up in your basement to beg your friends to buy. In addition, the POD company can do all the book production, get a Library of Congress number and an ISBN number for it to be sold though stores. They can help you with the cover and any graphics, proofing and printing. You will be charged a reasonable fee, according to a set plan or package.

Another advantage of the Print on Demand approach is that you do not need an agent. These are people who sell your book to a publisher. In this case you are going to shop around and evaluate what you consider to be the top five POD companies, go to their web sites, try and make sense of their services and packages, interview them and compare their approach and benefits.

Even if you write the book entirely yourself, you do need help from experts. If you want to present a finished product to the POD editor, you will need other essential people as part of your team. You might think you have outstanding desktop publishing skills and stupendous writing skills, but it is still wise to pass the book along to a communications expert, who can tweak and write in the style that your target market can relate to. Your team might include a desktop publisher for compilation of the master book and final formatting in a PDF file; a copy editor; an illustrator and graphic designer, and a researcher to help with any quotations sources and references you used.

Once submitted, the quality of paper, cover and printing itself are largely in the hands of the publisher.

You can stipulate how you want it to look, the font, the graphics, and the layout and choose the pantone color for the cover, but in my experience, they never come out exactly as you anticipate. There is a gremlin in the CD who tends to change things before the printer takes over and even he has no control over his machine!

Unless your name is King or Gresham, you have to market your own book, with or without a publisher's help. As

consultants, our best form of advertising is to do a seminar, a keynote speech, or workshop and sell the books at the back of the room.

You can also give your book to every client or every seminar participant and include it in the seminar fee. Another great way to sell your book is to attend association conferences. For example, the Association of Image Consultants International (AICI) has a conference bookstore where you can exhibit and sell your book. Links from your web site to those of others have proven useful in forming a huge international network and your book can then be bought online. Establishing a Pay Pal or a merchant account would make it possible for you to accept credit cards. If your book shows promising sales, your POD company can also get your book distributed by Amazon, Barnes and Noble, Ingram which sells to small retailers, or other independent distribution channels.

Marketing tips from VirtualBookWorm:

MARKET EVERYWHERE

Marketing your book is never easy. That's why it should also never cease. Hand out business cards with your web address, put the address (or even the order page from Virtualbookworm) on all your email signatures, holiday cards, etc. When your town has holiday festivals or town celebrations, rent a booth to autograph and sell your book. You look more important if someone else takes the money and you just sign and talk with your prospective readers. Place some autographed copies of your book on eBay, and make sure your sales page describes the details of the book so you get virtually free advertising.

Here are some other ideas:

1. Pens/pencils with your book sales page address.
2. Add your sales page address to fax cover sheets and other correspondence.
3. Donate a few autographed copies to local auctions, raffles and charities (especially your local

PBS affiliate, since it will get a number of mentions during their on-air auction).

4. Give your book as a Christmas gift to clients, neighbors, etc.
5. Ask your local library if you can conduct a reading.
6. Do readings for local civic groups, etc. and give free speeches on writing.
7. Ask gift shops, video stores and others (even convenience stores!) to sell your book.
8. Print postcards of you book cover and do a mass mailing.
9. Put some free copies (mark them as complimentary copies) in waiting rooms of local dentists and physicians (your book should hook readers to go buy a copy). You can even remove half of the book pages (again mark the book as such) so it won't get stolen for a free read.
10. Join every internet user group, etc. that interests you. Don't specifically mention the book (many will consider that spam);

include your web address or sales page in your signature line.

11. Create your own event! Call every television station within a 75-mile radius and ask to speak to the news director or a producer of the morning show (or any "light" variety show that isn't all news). Explain that you are a local author and ask if you can promote a book signing on-air with an appearance. If they answer in the affirmative, schedule it far in advance so you can now use this as leverage in your local chain bookstores. They will now be much more open to scheduling a signing since it will be mentioned on TV. If it doesn't work, get a mom-and-pop bookstore to do a signing. Once you have that down, now contact the local newspapers and mention the signing, TV appearance, etc. They definitely don't want to be left out and will probably write at least a small blurb. Or, you may

even hit a home run by getting a profile story written about you.

12. Don't forget the mall! Call the nearest ones and ask how much it would cost to rent a kiosk on the weekends. Set up your own signing (and maybe even have a mall bookstore help you) and create your own buzz.

Don't expect to retire on your book royalties! The purpose of a first-time book for a consultant is hardly ever to make money. It is more like a grand business card and gives you enormous credibility with trade associations, professional peers, your clients, and the general public. It establishes you as an industry or professional expert, which is a big advantage in the consulting or coaching professions when you can become a commodity very easily. The range of royalties paid to you by POD companies is 15% to 35% after their expenses. If you buy the books yourself, this royalty is passed on to you as a discount. (Publishing companies pay 6%-10% or less). Your book sales records always lag behind a month or two and you never quite know how well your book is selling, unless your POD company has an authors' on-line commissions page or communicates updated sales numbers with you regularly. The price of your book can be set by you and the publisher, but technical and niche market books are usually more expensive. Browse around a bookstore and compare retail prices of books like yours.

The Process for Self-Publishing

Write the book

Send it to a copy editor and other experts on your team for proofing and editing, illustrating and re-writing.

Research your top five POD companies.

- Send your manuscript (PDF formatted) to the POD company who shows the most interest. Go on down the line if the first one doesn't accept it.

- Get feedback and take their advice.

- Decide on the package you will need to get the book completed.

- Read the contract carefully and negotiate any points.

- Ask experts in your field to read the book and make back- cover comments.

- Design a cover or critique and select a cover design.

- Submit the book in a PDF file and send it on a CD to the POD Company.

Chapter 15

ASSOCIATIONS: YOUR EDUCATION, GROWTH, AND DEVELOPMENT

My first visit to AICI was in November 1992 in San Francisco. I had been in the fashion, education, and image business all my working life in one form or another and was curious to find out what the industry and the association were all about. During that conference, I had two important insights. First, I found out that the people who went into the image business were passionate about people, beauty, education and growth. The people I met there were enthusiastic, compassionate, pioneering spirits who had a vision to take on the image industry and grow it.

The second insight was that I wasn't, as I had imagined, a beginner in my field. Although I had quite a bit of experience at that point and had started to offer official training courses, I still considered myself new to the industry. At the AICI conference in 1992, I found out that we all felt that way!

I learned that two associations existed a few years previously, one west coast and one east coast and in 1990, they were combined under the very capable hands of a Merger Committee. I was impressed with the professionalism, fortitude, dogged persistence, and excellence of standards on which the new AICI was founded. For example, the original AICI Code of Ethics, which has served the Association, with very few revisions since its inception, is a document of policies and procedures from which many a corporation and organization could benefit.

Indeed that pioneer instinct to survive, to be recognized as an industry and to implement a vision, not to mention our desire to empower people, were very much the drivers of the Board of Directors during the 1990's. I was delighted to find so many visionary soul mates and jumped at the chance to be part of the International AICI Board in 1993. I joined as the VP-Education and what a steep but rewarding learning curve that was. Every year, the board had one face-to-face retreat, one board meeting at the annual conference and a monthly telephone conference call. The rest of the time, we were on our own. It turned out to be a lean but powerful structure on which to grow the association. I have never worked with people who were so dedicated, focused and visionary and can say with certainty that those who have taken committee and board positions at AICI still are to this day.

During that era of our growth, we were in the business of defining who we were and getting that message out to the public. We had a lot of work to do. Among other tasks we had to

- introduce business and other skills to our membership beyond our own areas of expertise
- expand our capacities of leadership
- set standards of educational excellence
- create levels of expertise

- market ourselves to a public that thought imaging was something medical!

By the time I left the board in 1997, Casual Business Image had swept though the country and corporations needed us to make sense of the epidemic. They were hiring us to help with guidelines and dress codes. We coached both individuals with potential and the executives who had been promoted. Even with fluctuations in the economy, we always seemed to be in demand. We were regularly appearing in the media and making a huge difference with our clients. By 2000, as an association, AICI came of age and in the new millennium, with the advent of the TV makeover programs, image consulting became a household term. The most recent years have seen a huge growth spurt for AICI in the direction of standards. As the membership grows in number and range of experience, so must the differentiation between beginners and experienced members be acknowledged and marketed to the public. AICI has been prescient in creating the current professional levels to which all members can stretch and advance.

Today, AICI is the largest professional association of personal and corporate image consultants worldwide. Over a third of the members live in 30 countries outside the United States and there are chapters in North America, S. America, Europe, Asia and Australia. AICI is an Authorized Provider of Continuing Education Units (CEUs) under the International Association for Continuing Education and Training. Each chapter and the annual conference provide educational and continuing professional development programs that offer approved CEUs.

AICI's core curriculum includes all aspects of image. Consulting for individual clients covers color, style, makeup and wardrobe analysis, shopping services, verbal and nonverbal communication, presentation skills, etiquette, self-branding and the total presence of an individual. Corporate image consulting includes seminars, workshops and individual coaching on branding, corporate identity design and customer service, as well as appearance, etiquette, verbal and nonverbal communication and business protocol. The curriculum also includes business development and entrepreneurial skills. To view the AICI Core Curriculum, see www.aici.org/education/core_curriculum.

Benefits of joining AICI

Networking

We are part of an international network. This became very apparent to me when the economy became increasingly global and my company went national then international. When I looked around for professional partners with whom to expand my business internationally, I approached the contacts and the network I knew and trusted through AICI. I also could refer any business from another city that came my way to local image consultants. They in turn referred back and eventually we have become this amazingly supportive community. I was always able to discuss my business problems with AICI associates many of whom have become life-long friends.

Committee Participation

In any association, the more you put in, the more you get out. It's the same with AICI. I took the board position as much to grow and develop my own skills as to grow and develop the industry. Both my self-interest and vision were fulfilled and satisfied through my work with AICI. Certainly, I spent long hours on the board, as the chair of the conferences, traveling many miles to retreats, sitting on tons of phone calls and sending countless fax messages. I grew to such an extent in leadership, management, presentation, time management and event planning skills that the benefits far outweighed the time spent. I remember at first being so scared to speak on conference calls that I had to write everything down in full sentences with stage directions, simply to remember what to say and how to say it! As President and Past President, I also dealt with some knotty problems, expanding ten-fold my communication capacities and the ability to handle tough conversations. When it came to managing my company and even my family, the problems paled at the complexity of the issues we faced daily, running a young association!

Conference Exhibits

The association also offers a vast array of exhibits during the annual conference. Here you can browse through the displays and speak with all the educators and consultants about their schools, training programs, designer clothes, color systems, manuals, videotapes, steam machines, skin care devices and accessories. It is a veritable smorgasbord of delicious opportunity to buy, compare and make friends. There is also a bookstore stacked with all the latest books on image and related subjects. Image consultants are always on the cutting edge of the latest in color systems, training methods, consulting tools and methods, designers and direct designer lines (sold by image consultants in their homes), body analysis tools and other accessories for our trade. The benefit is that you can find them all under one roof, at the annual conference.

Conference Education

In the early years of my career, I was anxious to learn everything and broaden my spectrum of skills. However, I couldn't afford to take every course, or buy every system. The conference allowed me to take short sessions from all the experienced masters, not only in our industry but also from other related professions, for a fraction of the cost to seek them out myself. I attended them all: Sales and marketing, color, style and body analysis sessions, etiquette, branding, nonverbal and verbal communication, coaching and leadership classes, media training, presentation skills and computer and Power Point courses. I wrote my portion of my first book from the tips from a session on book writing without tears! It was all exceptionally useful.

AICI Education Levels

You can join AICI at any stage of your career or without a career at all! As a full-time student, you even have a special rate. There are three levels of certification awarded by the Association. You are not required to take an exam or earn Continuing Education Units (CEUs) for membership. One CEU is awarded for .1 contact hour of education, so 10 contact hours would be 1 CEU. If you

don't have enough CEUs in any of the timeframes for any reason, you can make up the lapsed CEUs, pay a small processing fee, and have your previous level of certification status reinstated.

First Level of Certification (*FLC*)

This is a written exam, taken at the annual conference and planned for a few other exam centers in the world. Translators are available if your first language is not English. The exam tests whether you are familiar with the foundation topics of image consulting. You are required to earn three CEUs within a four-year period to maintain your First Level Certification (AICI,). The AICI web site provides you with a study guide and a booklist for your exam preparation and strongly recommends that at every opportunity you attend the conference, chapter education days and other authorized professional development to advance in your career. If you pass the exam, you are entitled to put AICI after your name in this way: Mary Smith, AICI. Check the ACI web site for updates on this designation.

Certified Image Professional (*CIP*)

You may apply for your CIP immediately after passing your FLC if you have the qualifications per the CIP application. This level requires you to submit a written 20- page application, divided into sections, documenting all your academic and professional education and training, your experience, promotional and marketing materials, and your participation with AICI or other leadership roles, for a total number of 1000 points. The minimum number of points must be demonstrated with proof for every section. The document can be downloaded from the web site: www.aici.org. You are required to earn three CEUs within a four-year period to maintain your Certified Image Professional status and can write your name in this way: Mary Smith, AICI, CIP.

Certified Image Master (*CIM*)

The Certified Image Master (AICI, CIM) reflects a high level of motivation, personal and professional achievement and demonstrates your commitment to the whole industry. You can declare yourself a CIM candidate after four years as a CIP, so it is recommended that you start preparing for this level as soon as you become a CIP and keep every scrap of proof of your client hours and proof of fees. The CIM level requires a portfolio of documentation, extending back five years before your candidacy year. The completed portfolio and the rest of your arsenal of materials are reviewed by two external reviewers. The CIM requirements stipulate that you must continue your education; serve in a leadership capacity in AICI or another organization; have proof of 1500 hours of paid work within five years preceding the application year; include in the portfolio any original materials such as programs, books, CD-ROMs, videos and marketing materials, and submit 20 client and peer evaluations. You will also have an interview by the CIM chair and will need to clear up any outstanding ethical issues, before you are awarded the CIM status. The decision rests in the hands of the committee and acceptance is not automatic. You will need four CEUs within a five-year period to maintain your status as a Certified Image Master and if accepted you can write your name in this way: Mary Smith, AICI, CIM.

AICI Sets the Industry Standard

There are many benefits to this hierarchical system, particularly in a new industry like image consulting. Since so many people have started their own entrepreneurial image businesses in the last few years and the general public has no idea the training and standards involved, it is important that AICI offers and establishes them. Any professional career path allows for growth and development and the image business is no different. Image Consulting in the United States has become by definition wider, deeper and covers a more in-depth consulting approach with clients than even five years ago. Image is now defined as "the inside and the outside" and AICI has set international industry standards so that its members can advance in their careers. Not only have we something to aim for, but we can also be rewarded for our efforts, education, technical knowledge and experience! Since image consulting is such a wide discipline, we can also educate employers and clients that we have kept abreast of current thinking in many different areas. Having standards and levels is a clear way of designating yourself as an image consultant, thereby distinguishing you from people who have minimal training.

First Level of Certification

The following section is purely an overview with recommended guidelines. Please visit the AICI web site for updated study guide, reading list and application. Click on Education and then the FLC section.

The FLC exam addresses the three major fields of image consulting for men and women in the US:

- Visual appearance and professional image presentation
- Verbal communication
- Nonverbal communication

Business ethics practices and professional presentation will also be covered. The AICI web site reference is the Code of Ethics http://www.aici.org/about/code.htm.

The exam is not asking for any specific philosophy or approach. The information you will need to learn is universal and many of the concepts are in the public domain. A booklist is provided from which the exam questions are based so it is wise to read at least some of the image and business books; invest in a credible training program, and have some practical experience before you take it.

Professional Ethics

The Professional Ethics sections require knowledge of the AICI Code of Ethics and contain questions on your obligations to the public, the client and to your professional association and colleagues. The exam is in "multiple choice" format. For instance, you will be given an everyday problem and three or four choices that describe the most appropriate solution. In the case of ethical situations, there may be no "right" answer but there may be one or two more obvious avenues to take, and either one would be accepted.

Business Practices

In the Business sections, the questions concentrate on your ability to build a credible business with goals and a business focus. You will be asked

questions on setting a professional fee structure, on communicating with all types of client, marketing, and maintaining your business, promoting your business services and products with clarity, and speaking with authority about your company. Since we teach people about professionalism, it is incumbent on us to walk the talk.

Core Knowledge of Color

As an image consultant, your essential core knowledge of color is based on the same body of distinctions determined by the fields of art and applied art. Art, interior design, fashion design, textiles and graphics all use the same principles, based on the hues of the color wheel. The FLC color sections test your knowledge of color properties, psychology and harmony. You will be asked to differentiate between properties such as: temperature, (warm and cool); value, (dark to light); intensity (high to low). You will need to be familiar with the terms chroma, saturation and color harmony patterns such as such as monochromatic, neutral, analogous, complimentary and triadic. Your knowledge of color qualities will be tested such as pure, washed, tinted, shaded, toasted and muted.

You will need to know the psychological effect and communication messages of the six hues, red, orange, yellow, green, blue, and violet.

The personal color information again, is similar to that of the art and interior design worlds. You will need to be familiar with the basic harmonies found in personal coloring, such as neutral, monochromatic, analogous, complimentary, and triadic, and the seasonal color systems: spring, summer, autumn, winter. An important sub set of personal color is the multi-ethnic coloring and color variation (value difference) in light to dark skins with which you will need to be familiar. Many color systems use different terminology so the exam makes allowances for many of these.

Body/Figure Analysis: Women

For the FLC you will need to be familiar with art principles as they relate to:

1. The human body: line, shape, proportion, body details, scale and texture.

2. Face shapes
3. Clothing design and garment construction:
    a. Silhouette: Rectangle, Oval/diamond/apple, Hourglass/low-hip, Figure eight/high-hip, Inverted triangle and Triangle/pear.
    b. Vertical and horizontal proportion
    c. Balance
    d. Scale
    e. Emphasis/repetition
    f. Harmony
    g. Techniques to camouflage/counter, or highlight/repeat

For men, you will need to know the three main body silhouettes and how best to clothe them: Rectangle, Oval/diamond/apple, Inverted triangle, Triangle/pear; Proportion and Face shapes.

Personal Style

Clothing preferences, fashion personalities and clothing styles are all similar terms for personal style. The image industry has adopted fairly uniform words for these concepts and you will need to be familiar with the main terminology and how to create a personal style for your client.

- Traditional/Tailored
- Classic/Elegant
- Sporty/Casual/Natural
- Romantic/Feminine
- Dramatic/High Fashion
- Creative
- Sexy/Alluring

Wardrobe Strategies

Many image consultants who deal with individuals are often asked to go through their clients' wardrobes and work with the actual organization of clothing, the structure and organization of a closet, garment choices and lifestyle needs. These are considered basic skills of an image consultant and your knowledge will be tested on the FLC exam.

You will need to know basic fabric knowledge and its care. You will have to evaluate basic clothing categories in terms of

a. Fashion: fashion, trend, and classic clothing styles

b. Clothing styles: Basics, classics, separates, tailored/untailored

c. Groupings of clothes: Clusters/capsules/units/modules

d. Personality and lifestyle.

You will need to know how to choose accessories to enhance facial structure, style, and character of the outfits.

Men's wardrobe requires a talent for pattern and color coordination; fabrication and styles of suits and shirts, body types and clothing styles.

Wardrobe: Business Dress

Wardrobe strategies for the business environment for both men and women require knowledge of business dress and business casual, and the levels of both. You will also need to know clothing options, fabrics, fit, accessories, grooming, hair and makeup appropriate to the business environment. Knowledge of specific industry standards will also be helpful.

Closet Clearing

You will need to work like a professional organizer if you attempt to work through a closet. The exam will test your ability to organize from very small to very large closets; evaluate clothing and clear out the non-essentials; help clients with storage and seasonal storage details, and clothing care.

Shopping Services

Some image consultants are also personal shoppers. You will need to know how to shop for individual clients and how to work with stores. Especially important is the knowledge of fit and the variations in fit of so-called standardized sizing!

Hair, Skin, Make-up

If you offer makeup, you will need to know how to work with warm and cool skin tones and a basic knowledge of skin types and skin care. You will need to know how makeup enhances and relates to personality, lifestyle, coloring, face shape and proportion. Although some states in the US do not allow makeup application without a cosmetology license, image consultants need to be sufficiently proficient in makeup application techniques and use of tools to advise and critique clients. Few of us cut hair but we need to know basic hair types and hair care and knowledge of hairstyles related to personality, face shape, body proportion, and lifestyle. As for grooming, we are often asked by organizations to consult on difficult issues such as body odor. We need to know how to deal with those and all other basic grooming standards.

Etiquette and Protocol

For the FLC, AICI requires that image consultants have a working knowledge of social and business introductions; gender etiquette by country (North America, Europe, Asia); high tech communication etiquette: telephone, fax, voice mail, email and dining etiquette such as table setting, menu recommendations, eating difficult foods, smoking and drinking, and professional business conduct. If you do not do that kind of work with your clients, you do not have to pass every section in the exam, but it would be worthwhile to read some appropriate books to broaden your services.

Body Language and Verbal Communication

Again, you might not be an expert but you might have a basic knowledge of the components of body language and verbal communication, such as posture, personal space, eye contact, body echoing and hand shakes. One or two good books on the subject will give you ample knowledge to make an attempt at any of the FLC questions in this section.

While the exam is divided into sections, the requirement for passing this exam is to achieve 70% correct from the total number of questions. You will *not* be required to pass each section. Some topics, due to the greater amount of information associated with them, will have more questions than other sections.

First Level Certification Reading List

The suggested reading list for the FLC exam on the AICI website is by no means a complete list of books that will facilitate your learning. There are many other resources available but the FLC exam is based on the *body of knowledge* contained in those books. The books were chosen based upon the following guidelines:

- Information is presented in a clear, concise manner
- Contents were geared toward the first level of learning
- Whenever possible, books were chosen that covered multiple FLC categories.
- Total number of books kept to a minimum
- Cost
- Easily available and current
- In print

The Federation of Image Consultants - TFIC

The Federation of Image Consultants was founded in 1988 as a national professional body in Britain to promote the image industry and standards of performance and good practice within the industry.

The benefits of membership are identical to AICI, with the main difference between the two being the methods used to establish and test standards. As we have seen, AICI has three levels of competence, which include an examination to test basic knowledge to become a first level Certified Image Consultant. TFIC, on the other hand developed a joint award with The City and Guilds of London Institute, an independent organization, operating under a Royal Charter, which enjoys wide support from many industries, working closely with the education service and government departments. Everyone joins TFIC as an affiliate member. As they progress in the industry, they can elect to take the TFIC, City and Guilds joint award to become

an Associate (AMFIC) and can become a Full Member, (MFIC). Full Members can be awarded the Fellowship of the Federation, (FFIC).

In seeking professional recognition for its members, TFIC developed standards of competence to provide a clear indication to both the industry and the public that the image industry as it was developed in Britain was serious in its aims and in its approach to business. It was essential to ensure that the standards would be understood by all image consultants, regardless of the methods by which they worked. Considerable research, consultation and observation were carried out to determine best practices and knowledge and ways in which these might objectively be assessed. The nationally based set of performance standards also establish ways in which professional image consultants could be easily identified by the public from those consultants who had not received or sought adequate training.

The City and Guilds of London

The award comprises practical assessments of candidates in a simulated working situation.

Each unit defines the key elements that constitute good practice of the subject and provide a core upon which consultants can build and develop their skills and raise their level of performance.

The Award is intended to provide a national qualification for the image industry and benefits clients and customers of the image industry who seek the assurance of a recognized qualification based on common standards of performance.

In addition to testing the knowledge of candidates, its also tests their ability to impart this knowledge to their clients which is a crucial requirement for a consultant.

The award tests both subject knowledge and proof of competence as candidates must take and pass the core unit and two optional units as follows:

Core unit:
- Colour Analysis

Optional units
- Style (Face & Figure Analysis) for Women
- Style (Face & Body Shape Analysis) for Men
- Instruction in Basic Cosmetic Application

To become a member of TFIC, contact info@tfic.org.uk.

The Last Word

There are enormous benefits to joining an association of your professional peers. First, you can establish where you fall in the formal and informal hierarchy. That knowledge allows you to examine candidly the training and the experience you need to grow and develop yourself. You can also ascertain where you can contribute, meet some friends and at the same time learn some skills. If you know you need skills in a certain area to grow your business, there is no safer place than to serve on a committee with your colleagues. An association offers a vast array of opportunities to hone your management and leadership skills, and if you want to grow your business, those are essential. Membership also helps you become comfortable mixing and mingling with your competition. The fear of competition is born from a mind-set of scarcity. Rest assured that there is work for all of us and each of us offers a unique set of skills.

As for me, I grew in humility as I grew my leadership muscles. That "know it all" persona, which I tried so carefully to hide reared its head from time to time at my first conference, not to mention my all time favorite, the "Mrs. Fix-It!" But, as soon as I was on a committee, I rolled up my sleeves and got to work with the best of them, I got a new appreciation for my peers and the job that my predecessors had taken on before me. For me, there was something magical to being on the court instead of in the stands: I was no longer an observer of life with all my assessments and opinions, but I was contributing to something I considered worthwhile. And while I was encountering the issues to resolve over there, I noticed that life became easier and a lot more fun. I was gaining wisdom and flourishing! I hope you will too.

Lynne Marks
2006

Printed in the United States
213465BV00001B/28/A